Janet S. S

Authenticity as an Executive Coach: Waking up the Wounded Healer Archetype

A book on the use and challenges of projection in Organizational Coaching

Book 2 in the Steinwedel Red Book Series

CHIRON PUBLICATIONS • ASHEVILLE, NORTH CAROLINA

www.ChironPublications.com

Second in the Steinwedel Red Book Series
Cover design and book typesetting by Cornelia G. Murariu
Cover artwork by Mariá Eva Trajterová

The key on the cover is the astrological symbol for the comet, Chiron, the Wounded Healer.

Printed primarily in the United States of America.

ISBN 978-1-63051-464-8 paperback
ISBN 978-1-63051-465-5 hardcover
ISBN 978-1-63051-466-2 electronic
ISBN 978-1-63051-467-9 limited edition paperback

Library of Congress Cataloging-in-Publication Data

Names:	Steinwedel, Janet S., author.
Title:	Authenticity as an executive coach : waking up the wounded healer archetype: a book on the use and challenges of projection in organizational coaching / Janet Steinwedel.
Description:	Asheville : Chiron Publications, [2018]	Series: Steinwedel red book series ; 2	Includes bibliographical references and index.
Identifiers:	LCCN 2017050409	ISBN 9781630514648 (pbk. : alk. paper)	ISBN 9781630514655 (hardcover : alk. paper)
Subjects:	LCSH: Executive coaching.	Mentoring in business.	Organizational learning.
Classification:	LCC HF5385 .S74 2018	DDC 658.4/07124--dc23 LC record available at https://lccn.loc.gov/2017050409

Praise for *Authenticity*

In this honest, self-aware and self-effacing work, Dr. Steinwedel offers the perspective of coaching as a journey meant to help both coach and coached become more fully themselves. In the process, she effectively expands on the notion of Coaching with an Analytical Framework from her earlier book, *The Golden Key to Executive Coaching*, adding additional insights gleaned from the perspective of the "wounded healer" archetype.

Fritz Haas, LPC
Clear Perspective

Steinwedel takes the complex and simplifies it to make Jung's theories immediately accessible to coaches allowing them to have greater awareness, clarity and impact in their next coaching session. This book illustrates the essential work coaches must do on themselves to bring more integrity to their coaching practice and the field of coaching.

Michael Nagle
Michael Nagle Consulting Group
Transformation Leadership Consultant and Executive Coach

I have known Dr. Steinwedel as a colleague and friend for over 15 years. As an executive coach she embodies both wisdom and pragmatism, developed through a commitment to her own personal journey of healing and growth.

Dr. Steinwedel's new book *Authenticity as an Executive Coach* is an insightful resource for the new or experienced coach to quickly identify potential traps and pitfalls that can arise in a coaching relationship. Steinwedel uses the "wounded healer" as a powerful model for personal exploration, understanding and working with clients to create healthy engagements, relationships, and growth focused solutions.

Roy A. Roper, MS,
Former CEO Delmarva Blood Bank

So many of the tropes of leadership set expectations that coaches need to be perfect people—they always need to have the answers. Steinwedel's work encourages coaches to think about the places in which they are wounded, as well as the ways in which they are healing, in order to authentically identify with themselves and others. By allowing coaches to honestly reflect on their whole person, her work creates space for coaches to truly fulfill their potential and to inspire this authenticity and effectiveness in others as well.

Katina Sawyer, PhD
Assistant Professor of Psychology
Graduate Programs in Human Resource Development
Villanova University

Table of Contents

Acknowledgments

I am particularly grateful to an ever-widening Jungian community that I now feel a significant connection with. Their openness and inclusivity has provided me with extremely rich and powerful personal and professional growth. I would especially like to thank Jim Hollis, Alden Josey, Sallie Bell, and the analysts at PAJA (The Philadelphia Jung Association); The C. G. Jung Institute Zurich in Kusnacht, Switzerland—where Shirley Ma, the only Chinese Jungian Analyst trained in Zurich, shared her work on footbinding (2005) and affected me deeply, initiating my interest in the Wounded Healer archetype—and The NY Center for Jungian Studies, along with its leaders, for their sincere commitment to the work they do in order to serve so many like me.

Dr. Hollis had just come back to the East Coast (Summer 2015) to lead the Washington Jung Center when we met for several hours to talk about the Wounded Healer in preparation for my beginning this writing. He is masterly in his understanding of human behavior and referencing of literary figures and motifs, as well as a joy to interact with.

For twenty years I've been delving into and enjoying poetry in parallel to my Jungian studies as a way to navigate emotions and to understand my self and my life more deeply. I am particularly grateful for the seminars and retreats provided by David Whyte. He has made poetry accessible and profoundly meaningful to me and in my work. I continuously draw on poems David has introduced me to, as well as many others over the years, to help my clients with a deeper understanding of their own experiences.

Great appreciation goes to Cara Lee Palmer and Jean Hauser who have trained me in mindfulness meditation, a great companion practice to poetry and analysis.

I want to acknowledge my clients for the opportunity they provide to me to keep learning with others who are in the crucible everyday. I'm grateful for their curiosity, courage, and sincere collaboration. Special appreciation goes to "Jennifer" who generously allowed me to use her Wounded Healer story.

Many thanks go to Anne Dubuisson, as an editor extraordinaire she held me accountable, kept me organized, and asked great questions to ensure a strong outcome.

Additionally, I am grateful to the team at Chiron Publications—Dr. Len Cruz, Dr. Steve Buser, Jennifer Fitzgerald, Nelly Murariu, Winifer Skattebol, and Katie Benfield— for kindly and skillfully managing all of the details of bringing this product to bear.

And finally my appreciation extends to family and friends, who have supported and challenged me on this journey, especially Steve, my husband of 20 years, who shares a love of poetry, the psycho-spiritual world, travel, and learning.

Br. David Steindl-Rast said, "Happiness is not what makes us grateful. It is gratefulness that makes us happy." I feel both grateful and happy as I bring this book to a close, appreciating new insights for myself and offering them up for whatever they may bring to the expansion of you, your work, and your life.

Dedicated to my Nieces

*Gabrielle ...as she heads off to college to
start her independent life*

Julia ...in her new marriage

*Wishing them great joy in their
search for authenticity*

Foreword

Executive coaching is an emerging profession which is still finding its way among many other consultative and therapeutic practices. It is the gift of Janet Steinwedel to titrate the insights of depth psychology and offer a sharper lens through which to see the common work. Jung pointed out that we can never take another person any further than we have traveled ourselves. Where we are stuck, our capacity to work with others will be stuck. Where we are caught in a complex, a defense, an avoidance, and old protection, our work with others is arrested. In her new book *Authenticity as an Executive Coach*, Steinwedel reminds the reader that before we can really be effective with others, we have to have worked on ourselves for a very long time. And continue to do so throughout our practice. This book brings insight, tools, and a refracting vision which helps the coach address the deeper currents present in our clients. So many of our therapies and practices address the visible world of choice and consequence, and ignore the invisible place from whence those choices have risen. Coaching in depth will require that the practitioner be able to track the movement of that invisible field of energy which courses through the visible world of choice, pattern, and consequence.

When we work with the other, the whole field of our own history of relationships is activated and in play, whether we know it or not. Where we historically felt overwhelmed by the circumstances of the other, we developed patterns of avoidance, power stratagems, or modes of compliance. Thus, when our own omnipresent history is evoked, we respond to the other inauthentically. Or, when we feel the potential loss or absence of the other, we may have our archaic coping mechanisms of self-devaluing, controlling behaviors, or inordinate neediness. Just as the history of the other is catalyzed in interpersonal relationships, so ours is as well. Despite our training and good intentions, where we are ignorant of our own psychological history—what it makes us do and what it keeps us from doing—we operate unconsciously in the interactive field with the other.

Steinwedel employs Jung's simple but complex diagram of the energy systems activated whenever we encounter the other, including how the unconscious of one injures the other or has a healing effect. When we realize that our own history of relationships is present in every encounter and colors our perception of the other, our styles of relating, and our hidden goals for the relationship, then we begin to realize the truth of Jung's warning that we cannot take others where we have not arrived ourselves.

Providing ample case examples and amplificatory material, Steinwedel gives a window into depth work with a client. As Terence observed two millennia ago, "nothing human is alien to me," so we see in the other the same hopes, fears, avoidances, secret shames, and self-reproach we have privately carried ourselves. Only when the coach can face this rugged terrain of the human soul can effective work, true presence to the other, be achieved. Talk is cheap. Where we are avoidant, so the unaddressed appears; where we are trying to make it "all right," the summons to grow in the other is thwarted through our intervention; where we are stuck in our own problems, so the problems of the others will weigh on us and lead to burnout, depression, self-medication, or to that false authority which arises out of self-doubt as compensation.

To further the reader's self-awareness, Steinwedel helpfully supplies a series of questions, the addressing of which brings the reader to greater personal awareness and greater clarity. Paradoxically, the more one can examine oneself, the more one can bear knowing oneself, the more one can find solace and personal forgiveness, the more authentically one can stand in the presence of the other. Whatever we put right in ourselves, wherever we have absorbed the wounds of history and grown from them, the better we are able to discern the wounded soul in clients and be present. We all learn techniques, but healing is the work of the deep psyche, the soul, and without that depth, technique remains superficial and sterile.

Recalling that the group is the sum of the individuals involved, including what is unconscious in each of them, Steinwedel also addresses the even more difficult task of group transformation. In all groups, the whole is stymied by the pathologies of the few. Where a narcissistic boss dominates, the system is ill, and soon, too, all those who serve it. Where the chain of authority is eroded, therein uncertainty, ambiguity, and doubt establish their foothold.

Similarly, just as each individual has a shadow, those parts of the personality one wishes to disown, so groups have shadows as well. Whatever is denied, whatever disowned, whatever projected on to others, comes back to the group in collective pathology and continuing troubled outcomes.

The most difficult of self-knowledge is self-acceptance, self-forgiveness. This work of knowing oneself is humbling, always humbling. Rather than emerge feeling superior to our past, or even superior to others, we find ourselves as flawed as the next person. But from this acknowledgment, and insight, much healing occurs. From this act of self-examination, great insight grows available to serve clients. When Socrates said that the unexamined life is not worth living, he reminded us that wheresoever are we blind, fearful, stuck, our work with others will be sabotaged. Wheresoever we have addressed the tasks which life brings us, there we will be true mentors, bridges, facilitators to our clients.

As Friedrich Nietzsche once observed over a century ago, "Who will teach the teachers?"—and we might add, "Who will heal the healers?" We can say that Steinwedel's summons to authenticity goes a long way to answer Nietzsche's question.

James Hollis, Ph.D.

James Hollis is a Jungian analyst in private practice in Washington, D.C. He is the author of 14 books, including Hauntings.

Preface

No, that's not what I'm saying.

No, that's not what I want.

Yes, that's what I've been trying to tell you.

You don't listen.

You're impatient.

He's not smart enough.

She's ahead of herself.

She's just not getting it.

He's a great guy, but...

Well, you know Jerry...

Do these statements sound familiar?

We all get caught up in the trappings of language, intention and unconsciousness daily...and likely many times in a day.

* * *

One cold winter day, two years ago, I was sitting in a meeting, listening to an older senior executive give me feedback about a leader in his organization. As he spoke, I found myself smiling; and I suddenly realized that I was calmly shaking my head in a knowing fashion at a comment he was making. With a start, I became dumbstruck. *Oh my. What did I just agree with?* The leader said, "I'm sure you can see her saying that." The *trick* wasn't overt. I'd say my nodding was a habit of listening. Not so much agreement as, "Yes, I heard you." But had I *really* heard? Not at first. I was on autopilot, taking notes. And yet, I was in collusion. I was unconsciously affirming my impression of this woman as one who is terse without conscious realization. This is what I'm referring to when I say "the trappings of language, intentions, and the unconscious." This was a projection from the leader with the [unconscious?] intent to lead me in a certain direction. Then a second one came…"But of course, you know *her*." I was more prepared this time—I didn't move my head an inch. I just raised my eyes and put on an insincere half-smile. It was as if I just got caught sneaking candy. Ugh, again, not the response I wanted to convey. I was relieved, however, to be catching these traps and wondered how many times I had failed to do so over the years. And then I wondered: how many times had *I* created such traps?

This book is meant to guide executive coaches (and additionally those in the teaching, counseling, and support professions) to recognize more of these entrapments. It is designed to enable us to make more effective choices through becoming more conscious, thereby ensuring that we engage in more skillful work with our clients. Consciousness is a function of our ego. What is not perceived by the ego is unconscious. When the ego works effectively with the Self (our inner guide) we have a more holistic perspective. More of the true personality evolves. We're able to have interactions with more integrity.

* * *

The Red Book Series

If you read Book One in this series, *The Golden Key to Executive Coaching*, you know that it was my studies in Jungian psychology over a 10-year period that led me to write about the integration of Jung's ideas and the work of the executive coach. This work builds on my understanding of adult learning and transformational development. And the work continues. I, by no means, want to suggest that I thoroughly *know* this body of work. It feels in many ways that I have merely scratched the surface. But in that scratching I can see a real value in committing myself to greater understanding of these ideas. I believe that coaches who continue to do their personal inner work at a deep level add exponential value to the leaders they engage with. My main goal is to inspire you to step into these murky waters of the psyche and forge your own way toward greater clarity in the world of coach-client relationships.

I also want to remind you of your own authority, that is, to encourage you to be more self-authoring. Or, as we often hear it stated today, to have authenticity in your work with your clients. To do this our knowing of what is true must come from a deep place, a place without imposition. The challenge is getting to that place.

C. G. Jung's *Red Book* was published in 2009, 50 years after his death. In this opus Jung described his "confrontations with the unconscious" as he sought to better understand people, personalities, and the inner life. He worked on the book for 16 years from 1914-1930. At the same time, he was further defining his theories of individuation and the development of the personality.

> "The growth of the mind is the widening of the range of consciousness, and … each step forward has been a most painful and laborious achievement."
>
> C.G. JUNG

In my own Red Book Series (in response to Jung's dictate that we all should have a red book), *The Golden Key to Executive Coaching* helps us understand "individuation" and that drive to uncover *who* we truly are and *what* we're truly meant to become. A "golden key" is an *archetypal* symbol of something that gives you access to a special place or to secret and noteworthy information. This second book in the Steinwedel Red Book Series highlights the communication between the coach and the coachee and the archetypal *Wounded Healer* that shows up in the relationship. In Greek mythology Chiron the centaur is known as the original Wounded Healer. In astrology, the key returns as the symbol of the comet Chiron. It symbolizes our deepest wound and our work to facilitate healing of that wound. This second book in the series, therefore, moves us into the topic of understanding and working with our wounds to better serve our clients and the Self[1].

We left the first book with the understanding of the need not only for attunement to our client but also, given the complexity of executive coaching, to the client's boss and organization, so that we don't miss so much of "what is" and can effectively navigate a way forward. Whereas we gave attention to self-awareness in the first book, in this one we turn our focus to being deeply attuned to ourselves in relationship with the coachee.

The Wounded Healer

Something that is archetypal brings an image to mind. That image reflects a set of opposites. When you picture a healer, you immediately picture a patient—someone in need of healing. We can't know up without down, light without dark, mother without father, masculine without feminine. To know one, we must know the other.

> "Wholeness is not achieved by cutting off a portion of one's being, but by integration of the contraries."
>
> CARL JUNG

We put our own cultural and personal spin on these archetypes, but the essence is the same for all people everywhere. When we add the reverse aspect of *wounded* to the healer we create a whole. Separated, split off, the healer (that is the doctor or, in our case, the coach) doesn't know (remember) what it is like to be wounded. He/she acts as if all that is known and embodied is healing. This can portray arrogance: an inability to listen or have empathy. Most people want a healer that can relate to them. To see the empathy in *her* eyes or hear it in *his* voice can make all the difference in believing that the healer knows something of *my* experience.

Jung felt himself to be a wounded healer because of the difficulty he experienced in childhood that drove him to his work as a doctor and analyst.

---

1   Self – Jung's use of the capital "S" Self was meant to differentiate from the ego self and focus in on a deeper resource available in all of us.

18

The archetype speaks to this need to help others because of our own wounding. Healing becomes a projection and the wounding often goes underground.

Proof of Heaven author, the neurosurgeon Eben Alexander, may also be considered a "wounded healer." After a coma, he became very aware of how differently he felt about his patients' experiences. He felt a responsibility to tell people about the afterlife he experienced in an effort to bring about a new kind of healing.

Then there are those like Oprah Winfrey. She was bullied and molested as a young girl and has gone on to make many contributions of a healing nature to her audiences and others.

The Psyche

Jung sources the word archetype to Plato, but it was Jung that created a school of psychology that would not exist without the word. Archetypes make up the collective unconscious, which is Jung's discovery (Table 1). The collective unconscious is an aspect of the psyche and is shared by all human beings.

TABLE 1 – PSYCHE MODEL

★ Complexes | ■ Archetypes

"But we owe to Jung the concept of the psychological archetypes: the characteristic patterns that pre-exist in the collective psyche of the human race, that repeat themselves eternally in the psyches of individual human beings and determine the basic ways that we perceive and function as psychological beings."

ROBERT JOHNSON
Inner Work

The *collective unconscious* is the inherited part of the psyche that holds knowledge from the beginning of time. Jung explained how he encountered the collective unconscious (also referred to as the "objective psyche") in his work with people's dreams. Various images would show up in a dream that a patient had no experience or knowledge of in his or her waking life—yet there it was in the dream—the unconscious realm, there to bring something of importance to consciousness.

Doing our inner work—connecting with the unconscious and our woundings—enables an integration of the opposites that results in an ability to be nimble and more resourceful in our work with others.

We all know people who have obvious wounds and you might have one yourself. Some are not so obvious. They may be the more emotional ones. All are significant and can have a lasting impact. When our wounds are ignored or repressed, they often show up in bad behavior. Perhaps you know very personally about these kinds of wounds.

We are all, quite frankly, wounded in some way and need to become aware of these wounds, no matter how inconsequential they may seem. These wounds form complexes (miniature personalities complete with *musts* and *shoulds*) in our psyches and often trigger negative energy (i.e., anger or resentment). They wear down our resilience. So even the leader who said, "And you know *her*," with some level of certainty that what he saw in her was something everyone could see, might have been reacting from a personal wound. That wounding may have formed a complex that he now projects outward in the form of demeaning or diminishing others. And I may have resonated with that wounding at some level myself, resulting in an *um hum*, a nod or a half smile.

Many people go into the healing and support professions because of their own wounds, but remain quite unaware of this. Being driven to help and bolster others because of an early wound that is relatively or totally unconscious is likely a balm for the wounded healer's pain. Yet we may carelessly project these very woundings onto others. For example, one female coach often spoke to me about the neediness of others, but it seemed to me that her own neediness was at the core of her unconscious concerns and behaviors. I later learned that she was often left alone as a child. She saw her mother as aloof and her father as the quintessential businessman. These are *her* projections.

Other times we see something in another person, potentially a client, which we dislike in ourselves. Noting that "he's so impatient" may be an opening for my own ability to see my impatience and how it is getting in my way. Herman Hesse, the Swiss poet, novelist and painter, said, "If you hate a person, you hate something in him that is part of yourself. What isn't part of ourselves doesn't disturb us."

Or perhaps we'll remember that in childhood we didn't like the critical nature of a parent and we've held it against him/her and others our whole lives. Who is affected more in such a situation, the offender or the one that holds the anger? There is a time when we must grow up and gain insight into what we've become and then discover who we would rather be.

And so our work in this book is not to merely look for sickness or wrongness, but to learn more deeply about ourselves, to enable our clients to learn more meaningfully about themselves. This in turn will alleviate some of the stress in our work lives and the various systems in which we go about living. It will strengthen our teams, make us and others more effective, and make our organizations more productive.

Navigating this Book

Drawing on the story of Chiron and other well-known wounded healers, I will naturally unravel my own tale of woundings and healings in the chapters ahead. I will also incorporate the stories of others. All the while I will continue to clarify Jungian ideas related to the psyche, individuation, and projection that are very important to our skillful work as executive coaches. Don't worry if you don't immediately understand these ideas; there will be more stories and information to further elucidate their meaning as you proceed.

In the last three of the nine years that I was working on *The Golden Key*, I was also thinking about the Wounded Healer. I started to give presentations on my ideas and to make notes about my own *woundings*[2] and the insights that ensued as they became more conscious. I hope that you will keep notes on your own wounded healer experiences as they unfold through your engagement in the chapters ahead. (As in the previous book, I've left a notes page for you.)

I have incorporated a host of poems that I collected during my work on this topic, which illuminate the book's ideas. Just as a picture paints a thousand words, so does poetry. It helps us to "get things" at a more visceral level.

I am reminded of a whimsical poem by Billy Collins called, "Introduction to Poetry." He starts by providing several ways to work with a poem and finishes with some frustration, noting,

> But all they want to do
> is tie the poem to a chair with a rope
> and torture a confession out of it.
> They begin beating it with a hose
> To find out what it really means.

I encourage you to keep reading at those times when you don't completely understand an idea. No need to torture a meaning out of any statement, it will come in time.

---

2   Some other words for considering woundings: Hurts, injuries, scars, harm, brokenness, disability, abuse, pain, etc.

I

Integrating the Archetype
of the Wounded Healer

To go through our wound is to embrace, assent, and say
"yes" to the mysteriously painful new place in ourselves
where the wound is leading us. Going through our wound,
we can allow ourselves to be re-created by the wound.
Our wound is not a static entity, but rather a continually
unfolding dynamic process that manifests, reveals and
incarnates itself through us, which is to say that our
wound is teaching us something about ourselves.

KARL KERENYI (Eranos seminars)

Who are you? Who are you *really*? Have you ever been depressed, oppressed, or repressed? Have you ever been sad, ashamed, or disappointed? Have you felt mad, hostile, jealous, irritated, or plain furious? Do you know what it means to be scared or insecure or to feel insignificant?

In his poem titled, "The Guest House," Rumi tells us, "This being human is a guest house, every morning a new arrival. A joy, a depression, a meanness..." then he exclaims: "Welcome and entertain them all, even if they're a crowd of sorrows....".

It's not the typical reaction to such [unwanted] guests. More than likely, we would try to rid ourselves of them rather quickly.

For those working in what tend to be called the "helping" or "caring" professions, it is particularly important to entertain such guests. It is important to get to know them and where they come from. To not know these feelings when they "enter our homes" means that we can't understand them in others. It means we are quite possibly projecting them on to others or even allowing them to cut us off from others.

Let's return to the question: "Who are you?" "Who Am I?" Put these words at the top of a blank piece of paper and list as many aspects of *who you are* as you possibly can. You might start with the simple (or common?) descriptions, *i.e.,* mother, daughter, sister, coach, father, son, brother, chemist. You might clarify some of these by noting, for example, mother of an autistic son, or father of twins, one of which died at birth.

As you push the question you might add other roles you play such as artist, runner, bon vivant, vegetarian, etc.

Now, consider which roles make you happiest, most satisfied, most grateful. Then note which roles have brought you the greatest *angst*, confusion, or pain. Which roles have brought you the most insight and personal growth? Are those the happiest ones or some of the more difficult ones? When you were listing your roles, did you include such things as, pessimist, depressive, contrarian, or other "negative" descriptors?

In his autobiography, Jung noted, "I am astonished, disappointed, pleased with myself. I am distressed, depressed, rapturous. I am all these things at once, and cannot add up the sum" (Jaffé 1989). What would be your sentence or two if you tried to sum up the identities and feelings that make up you? Can you be vulnerable enough to face all of the aspects within yourself?

We must know our self to share our self and to know what is appropriate to share in our various relationships. Sharing—opening our self to another—is the basis for relationship. Coach and coachee develop a special bond, yet there must be boundaries. We are often guiding our clients to develop stronger work relationships, and these, too, must be given boundaries.

Some clients (and some coaches) are slow to share their feelings—and often with good reason. The poet Goethe said, "Tell a wise person, or else keep silent, because the mass man will mock it right away." As each person learns about himself and accesses his depths, he needs a special confidant that can hear him and hold his thoughts while they are yet developing. If we are to be those wise people that others feel comfortable talking to, we must do our homework on our own emotional lives. Why are you a coach? How conscious are you? How aware are you of your own justifications, motives and feelings…your own responses and manipulations?

Goethe also asserts the importance of learning about ourselves: "And so long as you haven't experienced this: to die and so to grow, you are only a troubled guest on the dark earth." Here, death is metaphorical. We all must have many deaths during our lifetime. The child has to let go of childish ways (temper tantrums and a focus on "me"); adolescents have to separate from mom and dad (begin to imagine a life on their own, with a mate, possibly with children of their own).

> "Who looks outside, dreams; who looks inside awakens."
>
> CARL JUNG

Likewise, those endings (deaths) of what has been continue throughout our adult lives. We have to let go of some friends in order to move on. We have to divorce ourselves of some ambitions and interests in order to create a niche for ourselves. A job we expected to be great crashes and burns (death)…but it sets us up for a new, more appropriate opportunity we wouldn't have dreamed of before. When we look back over our lives, we should see a steady unfolding of experiences and awareness that brought us to *this* place.

Lessons from Wounded Healers

In Greek mythology, Chiron was great and strong, winning all the races in his community of centaurs. In one version of his story, there was a fateful day when Chiron was admiring one of Hercules arrows and dropped it on his foot (Brookes 1994). The arrow was laced with poison and the wound that formed could not be healed.

Day after day, Chiron walked around the forest hoping to find a cure for his wound. Feeling painful in each agonizing step he'd stop awhile to

25

rest here and there. As he whiled away his time, he developed a love and knowledge for the herbs and other healing plant life he came upon. He tried many things to heal his own wound—all for naught. Over the years, with help from Apollo and Artemis, he taught himself the art of healing others, but first, he had to accept the death of his speed and agility.

Continuing for a moment with our Greek mythology, I'd like to remind you of another healer, Asklepios, and some of the difficulties that strengthened and prepared him for his role. From day one, life wasn't easy for Asklepios. He was pulled from his mother's womb as she was being laid on a funeral pyre. His father, Apollo, didn't know quite what to do with him and took him to Chiron to be raised. During the many adventurous days he spent with Chiron, he learned the art of healing and how to cure his own wounds. Over time, Asklepios became a renowned physician, curing countless patients at his healing sanctuary at Epidaurus.

Another story of a wounded healer comes from a Thornton Wilder play called *The Angel That Troubled the Waters*. Wilder borrows from a Biblical story that takes place at the healing pools of Bethesda. In the story we are brought to a shadowy, gray cave where the "blind and malformed" seek cures. The physician asks to be cleansed and healed by the holy waters but the angel responds: "Stand back - this is not for you." Yet the physician is eager and presses forward. Again he pleads to be let down into the healing waters. But the angel is insistent...

> "Without your wound where would your power be? It is your very remorse that makes your low voice tremble into the hearts of men. The very angels themselves cannot persuade the wretched and blundering children on earth as can one human being broken on the wheels of living. In love's service only the wounded soldiers can serve. Draw back." (Collected Short Plays of Thornton Wilder, Volume 2, p. 71)

It is likely that you've had some suffering and challenge in your life. Go back for another look inside yourself and at those roles you noted earlier. Are there some new ones that have surfaced—some new troubled guests that appeared on your doorstep over the years?

While you may not have welcomed and entertained all of these visitors, as Rumi suggests, perhaps you can now see the value in your life's journey. How have your own experiences of suffering served you? No need to torture an answer out of yourself but be willing to hear the small voice that is rising from the depths.

Connecting with Shadow

Many coaches I know come from the field of Organizational Development. In an *OD Practitioner* article focusing on the self as an instrument, the author says:

> In practice, owning the self means devoting time and energy to learning about who we are, and how issues of family history, gender, race and sexuality affect self-perception. It means also identifying and exploring values by which we live our lives, as well as developing our intellectual, emotional, physical and spiritual capacities. (Cheung-Judge 2001)

In order to manage our lives, many of our sorrows and disappointments are relegated to the storage bin in our psyches, in what Jung called the personal unconscious. This becomes *shadow* material. Shadow is all the things we don't want to be aligned with. These are the things we often experience as weaknesses, shortcomings, and failures. They can be instincts, hurt feelings, and those experiences over which we despair. Jung said we all have shadow; it is what makes us human. It is in revisiting these shadow aspects at a pace and in a way that enables us to find value in them that

> "If you begin to understand what you are without trying to change it, then what you are undergoes a transformation."
>
> Jiddu Krishnamurti

we can integrate them for their highest purpose. The work of reflecting makes us better, stronger intra- and inter-relationally (intra- and inter-psychically, see Table 2, Analytical Communication Model, p. 32). If our stuff is oozing out in all directions or, conversely, all bound up, how can we work effectively with another person? Connecting with our wounded healer prepares us for all manner of conversations that might arise in the work we do.

"Everyone carries shadow and the less it is embodied in the individual's conscious life, the blacker and denser it is," Jung wrote. That was my impetus for writing *The Golden Key*, to share how we can incorporate truly transformational skills to enable more consciousness in our Self and our clients. When we accept our shadow, it gives us access, just like the right key in a lock. We gain access to our creativity and our greatness—not from an inflated standpoint, but from our own authority (Self). When we are self-authoring, we are able to do what we are here to do...we are healthily working toward our own individuation. Additionally, when we begin to integrate our shadow (this is lifelong work) we get connected to others—to all of humanity. This is the road to reconnecting with our wholeness. It is the journey we are all on.

Mindfulness expert and Director of the Stress Reduction Clinic at University of Massachusetts Memorial Health Care, Saki Santorelli, writes,

What would it be like to approach our lives, and to engage in the lives of others, knowing we are all inherently whole, intrinsically well, in need of being drawn forth into the discovery of unabashed completeness? How would this change the entire dance of practitioner and patient? What kind of relationship would be wrought and shaped when seen from, and uncompromisingly held within, this point of view? (Santorelli 1999)

Henry David Thoreau said that, "The mass of men lead lives of quiet desperation." But Jung felt this was so because people had no one to whom to tell their story.

Mary Oliver, in her poem "Wild Geese," makes this plea: "Tell me about despair, yours, and I will tell you mine. Meanwhile, the world goes on."

That is why our work as coaches, as facilitators of transformation, as empathic listeners, is so important to the individuals we work with and to the organizational culture of the places where they work. Indeed, the world goes on. The more people that engage with it and with each other at higher and higher levels, the better the outcomes will be.

In Book One, I mentioned how important dream work is to our developing more consciousness. It connects us with our shadow and with those aspects of our Self that are hard to see. Here is an example of a dream I had many years ago that I believe came to me for such benefit:

I am in a single bed that was nestled against the wall, under a window. Suddenly I feel an arm reaching toward me—it is pressing right through the screen in the window so that the screen becomes like a glove on the hand. It is reaching right toward me and I wake up with great relief. *But what was after me? What was that shadowy aspect?*

Jung used the techniques of *association* and *amplification* to work with dreams. The first thing to consider is what do I think of when I think of *hand* and *arm*? There are the personal associations of how I use *my* hands and arms, and there are the collective, or archetypal, associations, such as signing, eating, comforting, gesturing. To further amplify these thoughts, the arm is a very important tool in going about getting things done. We feed ourselves, care for others, and labor with our arms.

But this arm is "screened." When something has been screened I think of it as being reviewed, edited, checked out. I might consider if there are ways I am being handicapped because I have not made an effort. Have I not allowed myself to *embrace* an idea? How is it that I am not *reaching* my potential? Why was it coming toward me in the night? What did it want from me? It was powerful, it pushed right through the screen. Well, we could work on this for hours and we can learn from our dreams over years. Asklepios had his patients sleep at the sanctuary at Epidaurus. This enabled them to start their healing work with a fresh dream from the night before, providing inroads into understanding their illness.

Sometimes our shadow is *light* shadow and shows positive traits or talents. But these are relegated to shadow because they are gifts that went unacknowledged, or because we don't believe we can manifest them. The idea or ability may feel too big and too impossible for us to manage or be responsible for. But these also need to be integrated for our individuation and wholeness.

I often see a client's eyes fill up with tears when they feel stuck or their lives lack meaning. Many can't even say why exactly they feel sad. Some are just overwhelmed. In Jennifer's story in chapter 3, you will get more insight into what healing can look like for those that despair.

The Mission of a Coach

You might answer the question, Are you coaching, consulting, teaching or facilitating, with a "yes." We are often doing two or more of these in our client work. While many still think of our work as executive coaches as skill-building and fixing the negative aspects of a person, I think of it as freeing the individual to bring his/her unique blend of abilities to the fore. I am there to help remind people to reflect on their lives, their experiences, what really matters to them, and what they aspire to. I provide a mirror at times, a sounding board at other times, and sometimes I'm a container for their unconscious stuff. I support them in doing the deeper work that enables them to find their voice. And one important way of helping them find their voice is to listen deeply and share what I think I have heard, so that they can hear their words and feel how the message sits with them. I can call out inequities and paradoxes for further clarification, or just to be aware that they exist.

Ludwig Wittgenstein, a mathematician and philosopher, said, "We cannot enter any world for which we do not have the language." Our clients rely on us to teach them the language of growth and development, of leadership and authenticity. Coaches know that language best when they have traversed and made sense of similar difficulties. Understanding the ideas of individuation, consciousness, complexes, archetypes, and the experience of being human gives us a sense of what wholeness might look like and what brokenness can do to us.

I've learned important life lessons from my research, my work in organizations, and my various relationships. I've been committed to learning about my woundedness—my hurts and disappointments. The need to do this work may come from having a tender heart. I didn't know that was the case when I was young. I thought everyone had access to their feelings, but I was told regularly that I took things too personally and I cared too much. I can see that now that I've taken time to attend to my feelings—what I value—and to hold more of the painful side of life in my awareness without judgment. I can typically manage those feelings nowadays, but it is important that I get time to step back and gain more consciousness about situations as they arise. It has benefited me to stop and consider:

Why that response?

Why can't I let go of that feeling?

Why am I afraid?

Why do I make light of this or that?

"Wonder is the beginning of wisdom," Socrates said. Through my wondering and wanderings I see that everyone really does have a tender heart. Sometimes it is just hidden behind a wall or a door—protecting the fragile gift for another day. Perhaps it is waiting for just the right compassionate companion to come along and listen.

Unveiling the Backstory

Something is *often* happening in the room with a client… but much of it goes unnoticed. In *The Golden Key To Executive Coaching* I reviewed the analytical communication model (table 2). I introduce it again here, in order to set the stage for our work together in this book. Looking at the model, we see how communication wells up in the interactive field from the unconscious of either the coach or the client and makes an impact (positively or negatively) upon each's unconscious or consciousness.

"I engaged the "old man" in an interesting conversation. He said I treated thoughts as if I generated them myself, but thoughts are like animals in a forest, people in a room, or birds in the air. "If you see people in a room you don't say, you made those people, you're responsible for their existence." Only then did I learn "psychological objectivity." Only then could I say to a patient, "Be quiet, something is happening.""

C.G. JUNG

TABLE 2 – ANALYTICAL COMMUNICATION MODEL

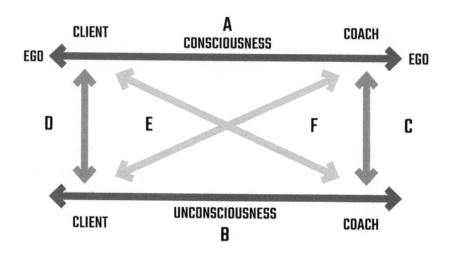

This is what we're here to talk about and make some sense of in our undertaking of the archetype of the Wounded Healer. It is called *projection*. As coaches (or analysts, therapists) in the room with the "Other" we speak of it as *transference* and *countertransference*. It is what you place on to me—*transfer* or *project*, and what I place on to you—*counter-transfer (project)*, that is not intentional and often not realized. I will share a number of examples throughout the book to help clarify what this looks like in the coaching relationship.

> "If I want to understand an individual human being, I must... adopt a completely new and unprejudiced attitude."
>
> C.G. JUNG

To provide a glimpse into how projection shows up, let's consider how, when we think that we know how to help the other person, we already have a precedent to draw upon. To know a person for such a short period of time and proclaim, "Yes, I can help" is fraught with projection. I am not suggesting that when you come out of that initial meeting with a potential client you say, "Well, gosh, I have no idea what to do." Yet it is critical to realize that anything you're thinking is a projection and that it will benefit you and your client if you stay curious and open to other options. We must continuously take a step back for another look at what is true and what is merely a possibility. Whenever you feel particularly sure of yourself, that should be a red flag.

Additionally, if you use assessment instruments, you might already be thinking about what style or type this person fits. Then you might have some sense of whether you like them or dislike them, if they're going to be easy or hard to work with, if you think they can be successful in this organization or not. This all happens quickly and often without intention. Taking the time to challenge your thoughts and reactions and consider what you attribute those ideas to from your history is key to cleaning up some of the projection.

When you actually have assessment results and face validity (and/or just time to reflect) you can see where you were off in your initial assumptions and in what you think you saw. For example, I might say, *I expected based on your initial comments that you were a very cautious, conservative type, but I don't see that in these results; do you ever experience yourself that way?* Or, *Based on first impressions it seems like we have a lot in common: I want to be sure we ascertain who you specifically are, the variances, the nuances that make you unique. Tell me more about how you got to this role and this organization and the difficulties and decisions you had to make along the way.*

Getting the backstory is critical. While you are not psychoanalyzing anyone, knowing about a person's joys, sorrows, losses, wins, *etc.* gives you context from which to ask further questions and get the clarification that helps you to manage projection. Getting some hint as to what emotions and experiences form the undercurrents to their aggression, passivity, pride, or shame gives you direction. It is also what creates the intimacy in the relationship that enables growth and transformation.

Realizing there is something always going on in one or both of you that is assumption or bias, based on beliefs and experiences, can move you to more clarity. Knowing there is always something shifting or coalescing allows you to leave space for what is not yet speech-ripe.

Projection and Power Needs

Remaining open and knowing that it is impossible to know with any certainty what is best for another helps us establish a relationship. Suggesting we know how to help a person shuts them down. Knowing is related to power—it puts us in a position of control: I know and you don't, and I can tell you if and when I choose. But when we learn *with* the other it makes for connection, as it brings together *logos* and *eros* (opposites). The author and well-known analyst Edward Edinger writes, "To be a knower means to dominate the known object by the power of Logos. To be the known one means to be the victim of the knower…However, the definition of consciousness as 'knowing with' has a second factor: it involves not only knowing but 'withness'." (Edinger 1984). This, Edinger notes, is the "dynamism of connectedness."

Many coaches like to think that they act out of selflessness, and that thought can feed the "power shadow." Most of us probably have one. Our work in large organizations with executives making good money and holding interesting and challenging jobs can certainly stimulate feelings of inflation. One Jungian analyst who wrote a book about social workers and analysts and their power shadow said that "the social worker feels obliged to regard the desire to help as his prime motivation. But in the depths of his soul the opposite is simultaneously constellated—not the desire to help, but the lust for power and joy in depotentiating the client" (Guggenbühl-Craig 1971). While this sounds harsh, we must look for these opposites, just because it is the very thing the ego does not want us to do. When one side of an idea falls into the darkness, it is likely to cause us problems. When we give it a hard look, we can recognize it, if even just a little, and then start to bring the opposites together for more meaningful outcomes.

Although we are often working with high-potential leaders, there are always areas for development. The manager or the HR leader may express a lot of good qualities about a coaching candidate, but the candidate usually also has a couple of issues surfacing that are starting to show up as potential blind spots. At this knowledge, the coach's ego may think, *okay, they need me, here's my opportunity to help, to look like a hero.* When we're willing to look at these feelings (I'm powerful, helpful, needed, smart...) for what they are, we can manage them. (Chapter Four targets questions we can ask ourselves in order to reflect and gain awareness of these shadow elements.)

One famed analyst, Jean Shinoda Bolen, M.D., suggests:

One way of contending with the shadow qualities of our work is to take a moment with each person, in every session to ask ourselves what we are seeing and therefore constellating in this person. What are we focusing on and therefore drawing out, and what are we ignoring or overlooking and therefore not giving credibility to? (Cruz and Buser 2016)

This is a good time to refer back to the exercise at the beginning of this chapter, "Who am I?" As you reviewed the roles you play and which roles are your favorites, what insights can you glean? Are these favorite roles similar in any way? Is there power or deference connected to these roles? Are you respected in these roles? Are they work roles or leisure roles? If all the roles you enjoy are helper roles, or service roles, how do they play out? What aspect of them makes you feel good? Are people dependent on your ability, your good nature, or your good ideas? In our work, the last thing we want to do is build dependent relationships. If we facilitate the process well and listen carefully, the clients' competence and self-knowledge guide them.

In the end, only the client can know how to heal and how to grow. We can't push them into it or sell them on an approach that would suit us. It is in the conversation, in the deep listening, that the resonant thought can become an insight for one or both parties. Jung referred to this empathic listening as the "attentive entering into the personality of the patient" (Jaffé 1989). It often has a lasting effect on both the client and the coach. It's easy to forget, especially if we're caught in our power shadow, that we too have the opportunity to gain insights for our own growth in these sessions, that we can be gaining healing and renewal through our work with our clients.

The Power of our Stories

Rumi says, "Keep walking, though there is no place to get to. Don't try to see through the distances. That's not for human beings…." Much of my client work is taking one step at a time, putting one foot in front of the other. It's a process of storytelling, making connections, and having revelations. In one HBR article on *Discovering Your Authentic Leadership*, the authors make an effort to describe how people become authentic leaders through understanding their stories. They note, "first and most important, they frame their life stories in ways that allow them to see themselves not as passive observers of their lives but rather as individuals who can develop self-awareness from their experiences" (George *et al.* 2007). The leaders emphasize living by one's values, the need to draw on a support network, and how they endeavor to live "integrated and grounded lives." The authors quote, "The story of your life is not your life. It is your story." Some of our stories don't come out as unequivocal facts of our history, but they are no less real and noteworthy.

Rumi goes on to say, "Move within, but don't move the way fear makes you move. Today like every other day, we wake up empty and frightened." Sounds like Thoreau's *living lives of quiet desperation*. And indeed, I have worked with clients that show signs of desperation. I know, however, that when "the helper" in me takes over I falter. But when I am conscious of my wounded healer—its strengths and its limitations—I can challenge my thoughts as well as those of my client, and we both prosper. Insights and self-awareness are critical to growth.

I have had clients who felt it was their "difficult bosses" who created their desperation. It is interesting to note that some of the harshest bosses are quite frightened and despairing. When we can see them differently and release our projection, it can help relieve some of the tension as well as make for a better relationship. We all—bosses, leaders, coaches—need for our stories to be heard, and we need to hear our stories. Listening to stories is our work. We develop our skillfulness through having a confidant to tell our own stories to. We can draw on the first two components of the Jungian model: *Confession,* and *Elucidation* (see appendix, page 107) described in *The Golden Key*, to solicit the story. When individuals first begin to tell their story it is like a *confession*—this is where I've been, this is what I've done. As the coach listens attentively and asks clarifying questions, insights arise and there is some *elucidation*. We also learn about ideas to hold and go back to at another time. Jung's idea of circumambulation is very important here. "...You replay the events and personal interactions that are important to your life, attempting to make sense of them to find your place in the world" (George et al. 2007). We must pay attention to how far a client can go in their confession at this time, but be aware of what would be of value to circle back to, inviting the client to tell us again, or tell us more, about that time. Our lives are a continuous circumambulation of our complexes and shadow. With each round we can see more, accept more, become more conscious, more integrated and balanced if we are open to it. Having a trusted companion to tell our stories to makes storytelling easier.

I still get surprised from time to time by the surfacing of my own wounds as a listener of stories, but this is the work of human development, and I am grateful for the opportunity to engage in this way.

We all have a story—you can count on that. Some people's stories make them project helpfulness and kindness (even when the listener might not want it). Some might project anger or impatience. When you find yourself

> "Where we have stopped dancing, singing, being enchanted by stories, or finding comfort in silence is where we have experienced the loss of soul. Dancing, singing, storytelling, and silence are the four universal healing salves."
>
> ANGELES ARRIEN

on the other side of someone's [inappropriate, unnecessary] desire to help, or someone's sharp tongue, stop and remember, there's a story behind this and it's likely a troubling one. It might do your tender heart some good... and it may even be of help to theirs.

Many stories start out as projections, and in asking good questions we're able to ferret out more information and maybe get some clarification. This is all tricky work—now we see it, now we don't. Sometimes the client will accept the invitation to go deeper, sometimes they won't. The thoughts and insights quickly go slip-sliding away. So in the next chapter we will focus on the idea of projection and understand how it shows up in the conversation between the coach and the client and how we can make use of it.

Your Notes

What are you feeling right now? What are you thinking? How will you make use of these feelings and thoughts?

_____

_____

_____

_____

_____

_____

_____

_____

_____

_____

_____

_____

_____

_____

_____

_____

_____

_____

_____

_____

_____

II

Projection, Transference, Counter-transference, and Transformation

Projections change the world into the replica of one's own unknown face.

C.G. JUNG

I met up with a coach colleague one day early in the spring, and she told me of the feelings she had for a client. She really fell for his cleverness—he was quick-witted, astute, and ingenious. Once she realized what captivated her, however, she knew she had some work to do. After some reflection and putting pieces together, she knew that she would have to take back the projection and reconnect with her own skillful adeptness. She did do this over a matter of 2-3 months, but it wasn't easy.

In the male-female relationship we often come into the realm of the *anima* and *animus* archetypes. The male who falls in love with a female client or colleague might be experiencing a muse (an anima figure). The female attracted to a male client may see this person, or his style, as fulfilling a need or providing a solution to a problem (an animus figure). This attraction is likely more about something creative in the coach/ person that needs to be set free, to be birthed and integrated toward wholeness. Anima and Animus (Archetypes) are part of the collective unconscious realm (See Psyche, Table 1). They are projections from our inner selves onto the other. When we make them conscious they bring us an opportunity to transform.

In my many interviews with coaches I typically ask why they go into this work. Many say they like helping others, they like helping the underdog, or they want to see well-intentioned people become successful. Some bemoan the fact that they didn't get that kind of support in their families, in their classrooms, or in their early work experiences. Others have felt very hurt by difficult experiences they couldn't fix. And some are simply entrepreneurs who like spending time with people discussing business.

In some instances, people express that it is a model they were very familiar with: *I was the eldest sibling and was taking care of people my whole childhood*; or, *My parents were both in the helping professions, it's really all I know*; or, *Both parents worked full-time and I had to learn things quickly and take care of myself.*

While many people have acknowledged and worked with these realities, many have not. The emotions are often blocked and projected outward. If I felt bullied, am I always trying to get back at bullies through my support of clients? If I was the underdog, do I have a bias about those who seem *naturally* successful? If I was a top dog, do I feel the need to make my client into a towering success (another notch in my own belt)?

Marriage is often a good place to learn about our projections. We tend to project what we need or want, what we care about and what we expect the "Other" to care about. The wife may want more affirmation and project a neediness the husband eschews. The husband might tell his wife she's selfish, but only because of his own desire for more opportunities to escape the mounting responsibilities in life.

Our projections carry into our work experiences as well. For example, a colleague who early in my career helped me develop my confidence and early success was someone upon whom I projected a great deal of admiration. Another colleague I had difficulty with was sloppy in dress and work style. My initial projection was that he wasn't effective. That wasn't the case. I had to own my projection of "sloppy" and think about why it was always so important for me to be neat and organized. In fact, finding "sloppy" was effective in helping me realize new ways to "let go."

In an effort to gain more personal consciousness, can you put your finger on some of your projections? You can find them by paying attention to your blaming, anger, annoyance, and even to your blissful happiness. What challenges might they have brought to you? How can you be more aware of the projections you make at home and in your work relationships? Practicing this level of awareness can bring greater clarity to where emotional growth is needed, resulting in more precise intention and higher degrees of relational satisfaction.

"The mirror does not flatter, it faithfully shows whatever looks into it; namely, the face we never show to the world because we cover it with the persona, the mask of the actor."

C. G. JUNG

It wasn't Jung's intention to merely point out where one was sick or struggling. He saw all of these issues or malfunctions as symptoms and suggestions that something needed to be expressed. "The general psychological reason for projection is always an activated unconscious that seeks expression" (Jung 1989). Sometimes it seeks affirmation for "being right." Sometimes it wants to be noticed, heard, to feel alive. Sometimes it wants to express fear.

We must realize that there are important messages to be heard in the projections. They are invitations, just as much as when Mary Oliver says, "Tell me about despair: yours, and I will tell you mine." This is the very mutual feeling of wanting relationship. We don't often go to such depths in the coaching relationship, but I have had just a couple of relationships move into that realm long after engagements were complete. There was a mutual projection of some interests, ideas and needs that connected us. Those projections led to a conscious invitation of friendship.

"Out beyond the ideas of wrongdoing and rightdoing there is a field. I will meet you there..."

RUMI

From the analytic frame, Jung referred to a *dialectical process:* a dialogic approach where there is mutuality. "Thus the analyst cannot simply use whatever authority he might possess, for he is 'in' the treatment just as much as the patient and it will be his development as a person rather than his knowledge that will be decisive" (Samuels *et al*). It is this work that we do here that matters most, not the additional degree, not yet another course that develops your IQ. That is not what will enable us to adapt to another person's psychic reality or to see our own. If we could outright say: *tell me about your needs and wants and I will tell you mine*, we wouldn't have to dance around projection. But that is our developmental work—for all of us.

Did I Say That?

At times our clients will transfer something on to us in our coaching role—a frustration, or an expectation, and we will react with annoyance or defensiveness. This response is known as "counter-transference." One client told me I was too busy when we had difficulty scheduling an appointment. I snapped back, *"As if you're not?"* Oops.

I once found myself angry with a senior executive for not telling me of an action that was about to come down in his organization. Had I known it, I could have helped my client handle it better. I didn't realize I was angry until after I gave him some feedback. I gave the feedback nicely enough (I'm a *nice* girl—one of *my* complexes) but I wanted him to understand that he could have alleviated a mess just by keeping me in the loop. When I stopped to reflect on it all I realized he actually did me a favor, since it involved a termination and I wouldn't have been able to talk about it if I did know. My anger was coming not only from my being left out but also from my inability to assuage the pain of my client. It rendered me helpless. This is the antithesis of what I project out: "I'm the kind of person who is helpful." Ugh. As soon as I hear it there is momentary disappointment and then a smile of recognition...*I resemble that remark.* I am a recovering helpful person. And you? From what are you in perpetual recovery?

A coach colleague told me of a time he showed up for a client meeting, only to find that the individual double-scheduled himself and couldn't meet with him. My colleague said he was so annoyed that he blurted out, "You have got to get your act together." When he stopped to think about what he said, he realized he was as much talking to himself as his client. He noted that he was at a point in which he was overburdened and didn't have time to confirm and check on things and was just running from one thing to the next. He felt this confrontation was a clear challenge to himself to start shedding some commitments.

In another instance, I was listening to a client talk about her boss. I knew her boss and knew that she was a difficult person…or at least that was *my* projection. I found myself empathizing in a way that was not useful. As these feelings became conscious to me, I was able to shift the dialogue around and come back to our real work. The real work at that moment, however, was to help my client recognize her own difficult nature. And later, in my personal reflection, it was for me to consider the difficult side of myself, or why I find it a personal infringement when people are seemingly difficult.

In psychology it is often noted that, "there is a hook to hang it on." So, perhaps this boss *does* seem to show a difficult personality (the hook), yet it is necessary to realize that is not the whole story. It is likely also difficult for me and for my client because of something in us. In this particular incident my client felt the boss was intimidating. My projection was that she was a "know-it-all." These were two different ways of seeing the issue, and they provided insight for each of us to take under consideration.

> Contemporary analytical psychology has deepened this interest of Jung's in countertransference. Fordham (1957) proposed that an analyst may be so in tune with his patient's inner world that he finds himself feeling or behaving in a way which he can see, with later understanding, is but an extension of his patient's intrapsychic processes projected into him. (Samuels, Shorter, and Plaut 1986)

The questions in Chapter Four will support your effort to be more conscious of this intermingling of psychic processes. Surely, in the coaching environment, we can't do depth work with every comment or reaction. I merely want to impress upon you the value of these kinds of insights and prepare you for the inter- and intra-psychic processes we're swimming in at any given time.

Coach as Container

Perhaps most often, we think of transference as the exchange that includes a client's treating you like a guru or psychotherapist, developing a dependency on you, or idealizing you as someone they have been close to in their life.

One such client lost her mother many years before we met. They had had a close relationship and the mother provided her daughter with great wisdom and direction in early adulthood. My client missed their regular conversations. At some point in our work, I began to feel the expectation for motherly support. Once I recognized it, I found opportunities in our meetings to ensure we engaged differently. For example, I clarified that calls between our meetings were only for urgent conversations and when I felt her getting chatty I moved us back to intentionality.

One of the most challenging differences for us as coaches (from the analytic experience) is that our clients call us, we meet up with them in the hallways of their workplaces, and our meetings take place in any variety of conference rooms, offices and touch-down spaces. This makes it difficult to manage the container and boundaries. Some clients will buy you a coffee at the company coffee bar, or you might pick up one for them on the way to their office. Once in your meeting, phones ring, texts ping, and people knock at the door. As much as we try for something resembling a *temenos,* it is often a more harried environment that results in fewer boundaries. One young woman I was working with had tears close to spilling over, but we were in a room with a glass door and she couldn't let go. The safety she needed wasn't available, and I felt restricted in my ability to encourage her to exhale and let the tears roll. We lost that moment and her stoicism prevailed. It took months for us to recover and recognize what stress was doing to her. In another instance, a man in his 50's and I were discussing the reality of his lost promotion; he was unusually pensive and beginning to engage in a really constructive way when he got pinged. The distraction of reading the message on his phone broke his introspection, bringing back the *persona,* resuming the ego's control. He said, "I just need to respond to this"…and that ended the thoughtful reflection we were engaged in. He was so close to connecting with his inner healer. It's in these moments, pregnant with transformative possibilities, that you wish your clients could meet you off-site in a quiet, contained space. And yet, as the container for all that happens in sessions with our clients, we can sometimes bring back these important moments at future times with our clients. I have used articles, poetry, and stories to aid me in this intention.

Transformation Comes with High-Value Work

We only extract the highest value when we, too, are open to learning and when we're exquisitely attentive. The insights thus produced bring us greater consciousness and give us a view into our complexes, assisting us in responding more effectively in future situations. You might remember a bit about complexes from reading *The Golden Key*. Complexes are those split-off parts of our selves that Jung called "splinter psyches." They are composed of images and ideas at the core of which is an archetype, such as the wounded healer. They are aspects that we don't like to recognize. However, if we show them just a glimmer of interest, they can make us more self-aware, giving us the opportunity to manage ourselves more effectively.

While our self-concept tends to filter out what we don't want to see, when we get triggered it is all right there in front of us. Seeing it and doing our reflective work enables ego-Self development. We're no longer just projecting it out there irresponsibly, but looking inside to see why it is happening and what is really going on. You'll get more ideas and practice on how to have this internal dialogue in Chapter Four. It is very useful to discuss this material with your own coach or analyst as we are uniquely blind to our own stuff. A little support and challenge from someone we trust is invaluable.

The maturity that comes from insight increases the value of the work we're currently engaged in and the work yet to come. It provides a new level of trust and confidence. It enables the change that takes us to higher levels of perception and thought and simplifies what formerly seemed complex.

It should be clear that transference/counter-transference is happening all the time. It is how we come to communicate. There would be very little said if there wasn't any projection. In discussing the value of analytic work and the ways in which it has typically been devalued, Robert Langs notes:

> … most of the presentations relate material about the patient, while virtually never mentioning anything about the analyst—unless the paper deals with counter-transference issues.

> … when they get into counter-transference, they do it as if its expressions were sporadic, occasional, instead of part of the continuous

communicative flow. Counter-transference is seen as blatantly cropping up from time to time, and as something to be rid of. It is not seen as inevitably present in every silence and intervention, as part of the continuous interaction, and as something to be mastered, minimized, and always recognized, especially in its more subtle or chronic, easily missed expressions. (Langs and Searles 1980)

I believe that many coaching certifications emphasize a questioning technique in an attempt to manage the "problem" of projection. But even our questions are a projection of what we think is important or how we want to direct the client. While we must not try to be analysts, my transformational approach to coaching, "CAF"—Coaching with an Analytical Framework (outlined in *The Golden Key*, see appendix for model)—marginally aligns with Jung's approach to analysis in an effort to create the space for honest relationship, deep growth, and sustainable development. If we only do this work for ourselves, not trying to integrate it with our client work, it will still have an impact on our effectiveness. We can then begin to understand the rule of "first do no harm." It is incumbent upon us to gain insight into our emotions, how they are useful to the work we are doing, and how they can muddy the waters. Being aware of the cast of characters (aspects of ourselves) that lie below the surface increases our self-awareness, our ability to self-manage, and our overall potency in this work of support and challenge. The coach who is not comfortable with emotions and steamrolls over the feelings of his clients or directs the conversation to an intellectual one when emotions arise can bring further harm to the client. These practitioners are in fact saying, *bury the emotions, that's not appropriate.* That probably only affirms what the person learned early in his life. Jung said, "The therapist must at all times keep watch over himself...over the way he is reacting to his patient," and notes the therapist must ask, "What does the patient mean to me?... The doctor is effective only when he himself is affected" (Sedgwick 1994).

Raw Intuition or Highly Directed, What's Your Approach?

Sometimes I really feel like I know where I'm going with a client. I have a plan for our time together and sometimes things even seem to flow in that planned direction for some period of time. But more often, the conversation splinters off into what is most important to the client in the moment. I believe that being flexible and nimble enough to follow a path that we are co-creating through our conversation is a necessity. This can make it hard in the corporate world where some want a specific proposal and a strategy and updates on the outcomes. But that is not transformational development. It is not realistic and it is really not possible if you believe the other person has value, purpose, and a contribution to make in their own development. You can always come back to a bifurcation and ask, "Do we need to explore this other branch?" Of course, if the answer is no, you may want to take a moment to explore "why," to ensure that it is not the ego's way of sneaking out of a tough conversation.

Listen to those "No's" in your own head as well. When you make a decision not to ask a question or make a point, be sure to ask yourself why you made that decision and push beyond the first rational explanation. In one situation, I was working with a female, senior level administrator on some issues she was relaying relative to her family of origin. She was on the verge of tears and I decided to ask her a question that would move us away from that tender space and allow her to get her composure back. Later, when I was reviewing the conversation and reflecting on her emotions and how they affected me, I began to question if that was the best decision. I have become quite comfortable with tears and yet this was only our first meeting. She was fighting with her emotions and I could see she really didn't want to cry (my projection, of course). But how do I know that that release wouldn't have been just what she needed? If she could cry in a safe place, might that have provided great refreshment, moving her toward some renewal rather than staying in this stuck place? Maybe it was *me* I was trying to keep safe, comfortable. How did I relate to the pain she was expressing? Was it too close to my own pain? I decided that if it came to this point in a subsequent meeting, I would allow her the space for that release. But now, I had to be aware of another counter-transference. I couldn't *make* this happen—it had to occur naturally. I couldn't thrust upon her the need for release of emotions—maybe it was momentary and wouldn't be applicable at the next meeting, at least not in the way that it was at that first meeting.

In counseling or therapy, it is more appropriate to go back and reflect on emotions and draw those emotions out. In coaching, it is more appropriate to move forward toward goals and aspirations. My work is intended to be transformational not just transactional, which requires some work with emotions.

Karolyi Kerenyi, a colleague of Jung's who regularly attended and presented at the Eranos lectures, sheds light on these particular moments. He notes that the wounded healer refers psychologically to the capacity "to be at home in the darkness of suffering and there to find germs of light and recovery with which, as though by enchantment, to bring forth Asklepios, the sunlike healer" (Mauger 2013). Additionally, he says:

> This archetype reveals to us that it is only by being willing to face, consciously experience and go through our wound that we receive its blessing. To go through the wound is to embrace, assent, and say "yes" to the mysteriously painful new place in ourselves where the wound is leading us. (Levy 2007)

Emoting and telling our stories are often initiatory processes that enable us to move on. We pass through the darkness and experience hope again. These mini-deaths unburden us and ready us to take on new things. Creativity returns and new ideas can be birthed. This is the nature of transformational growth. This is the space in which I work best…probably because as a wounded healer, I've been in the process of recovery and renewal myself.

Projection and the Challenge of Multiple Sponsors

Bullying is epic. We are talking about it today in many contexts. Sometimes it comes from parent to child, from a school experience, in church, in our work life, from the president of an institution or nation, between nations. Bullying does harm and it creates narcissistic wounding. This simply means a wounding to one's self-worth. And the bully is usually one that has been deeply hurt.

In one situation where I was asked to coach a bright, accomplished woman, I found myself smack in the middle of a bullying situation. In retrospect, I should have never taken the work. It was a trap. I had some underlying sense of that in the first meeting with the HR manager, the coachee's new manager, and his boss. They all sounded so empathetic, concerned, supportive, but they were really looking for my client to be fixed or to leave. We all know that hindsight is 20-20 vision, right? Now, some years later, as I think about all of the players (and several others surfaced over the year we worked together), I am sure that they were all working out of their own wounds. None of them could accept anything close to constructive feedback. They only wanted to hear about or reframe things as it related to them from a positive angle. They acted like what my mother would have called *spoiled brats*.

There I was caught with my client, who was being bullied from all directions. At first it seemed that she had the empathy of others for some abuse she had received from a senior leader. But she soon was re-victimized by those very same people. I tried to keep her focused on her own development and for a while it was working. She was progressing with her own insights and trying new ways of interacting at all levels in the organization. Soon, however, it became apparent that one particular co-worker wasn't happy with her progress. I think it was a matter of my client's being much smarter and more accomplished than the individual that set things in motion.

It is likely you detect projections in this story. I'm sure you can tear this case apart with the possible alternative stories that might have existed. I can and have, as I've reflected on it many times. All we can work with is what we have access to at the time. So, if we go back to Table 2, page 32, and look at the way in which information can get twisted in spaghetti-like confusion, we can consider that at any time in this work, there was a myriad of stuff coming from the unconscious parts of the participants. They were saying things at the "A" level of consciousness, but there was also a lot going on (projected) at the "B" level of unconsciousness. Some of that was being projected upward from unconsciousness in the direction of the "Other." To add to that conceivable mess there were usually three or four people involved at any given time. Each with his/her own individuation process and level of influence and power.

If we attempt to sum this up in relation to the Analytical Communication Model, what was going on at the conscious level "A" was input from the boss, two of the bosses' peers, the bosses' boss, the HR person, and my client as to what she needed to work on. That was a lot of contribution toward the development plan, but they all seemed to have good intentions and my client wanted to have their support. The client (conscious)-client (unconscious) line "D" represents what my client thought was the problem, and what she wanted to work on, in tension with what her ego was comfortable maintaining in the form of her persona.

The coach (conscious)-coach (unconscious) line "C" refers to my understanding of the situation and what is coming up from the unconscious that constellates my wounded healer and the picture I'm pulling together of my client. In this case, I was *feeling into* my client's experience of being bullied compounded by my own experiences of bullies. My empathy (sympathy?) level got too high at one point and I missed the shift (from being supportive of my client to being impatient with her) coming from a key sponsor.

Finally, the "E" and "F" lines represent what happens between two people forming a relationship. For the two of us, we bonded nicely. I'd say we liked each other, trusted each other. (We are *who* we are due to what is happening in the relationship... "what you're doing to me" and "what I'm doing to you" (consciously and unconsciously). And I listened a lot, supported, and carefully challenged (so that she could hear the message I was hearing and take it in to work with it) and learned a lot about her (committed worker, smart, experienced, difficult parental relationships, yet committed to her parents in their old age, and perhaps a bit fragile). At some point, she got too confident that she was right and her sponsors, in fact, were wrong. She then brought others into *the conversation* about what was going on in our coaching work, specifically where she was stuck on a particular issue involving some colleagues. She felt that in this way, she would have more support against the bullying. She achieved her goal, temporarily, but then too many people were in the soup and there was a big negative shift. Then the container was usurped by an outsider to the original cast of characters (most important, she and I) and things got very messy. It was a very educational experience for both of us, but also very disappointing. It has both haunted me and helped me over the ensuing years.

As I look back, from that first meeting with all of her "sponsors," there was an unbalanced polarity of the wounded healer archetype. She was the wounded, "unknowing" one and accepted that, and we were the healthy, "knowing" ones. The sponsors all knew very well what she needed to fix and they had no vulnerabilities. I was paying attention and taking in the "what went wrong/what needed to happen to alleviate the tension" scenario and was complicit in the "they (we) *vs.* her" set-up. The inflation from the group and the willing victim (deflated) were in place. In the end the only way for her to get out of that "less than" position was to thrust herself into *knowing*. This grand inflation did her in, because now she wasn't wrong about *anything*. In fact, she thought she was right about *everything*. If we draw on mythology, as Jungians often do, Icarus got too close to the sun and melted. This is what can happen when each of us doesn't take responsibility for both sides of the archetypal pole—in this case the wounded/vulnerable aspects of ourselves, along with the healer/knowing parts of ourselves.

Take a moment to consider some of your own experiences. Which ones got particularly messy—out of balance or out of control? Can you see your own projections in these situations? Were you vulnerable or invulnerable? Can you see how some of those projections came from the bullied, hurt aspects of yourself? What in particular was resonant? Where was your empathy (sympathy?) greatest? Again, in order to become more skilled, to be a better guide on the journey with others, we must look at ourselves. We must hold up the mirror and see what morsels of truth exist for us to learn from.

Poet Marina Tsvetaeva, in the early 1900's, wrote: "I know the truth – give up all other truths!" There are times when the truth seems so clear. Like those nights when we look up at a clear, dark sky and the stars are so vivid they pop with a tenaciousness that won't let them be ignored. When my client in the above story said to me, "I'm in a corner, there's no way out but to leave or be subservient," I felt such a truth. Tsvetaeva finishes the poem with a line that reverberates forever… "And soon all of us will sleep under the earth, we who never let each other sleep above it."

Sharing our stories, telling our truths in the "I – Thou" philosophy of Martin Buber, engages us in both sides of the archetypal pole: the desire to truly know another in their despair, with the knowing that only comes because being in touch with our own despair is true compassion (etymology: "to suffer with"). The next chapter illustrates this compassion through the story of a female doctor in the midst of her suffering.

Your Notes

What's up for you right now? What are you feeling in your body? What do you want to do as a result of your thoughts and feelings? What new insights do you have?

III

Jennifer's Story

*A sacred illness is one that educates us and
alters us from the inside out, provides experiences and
therefore knowledge that we could not possibly
achieve in any other way.*

DEENA METZGER

Jennifer was an emergency room physician on the rise when I first met her. She was in line for the Chair role because of her overall effectiveness. She was considered smart, competent, and responsive. She was energetic and confident, as demonstrated in her pace and in her dress. Not only did she work the crazy hours of an ER doc, but she was also committed to taking part in triathlons, was a wife, and also a mother to a teenage daughter. Her colleagues respected her.

Our first meeting was focused on reviewing three assessments: MBTI® *Step II*™ (Myers Briggs Type Indicator re: personality), VAL® (Values Arrangement List) and FIRO-B® (Fundamental Interpersonal Relations Orientation-Behavior/needs assessment) in preparation for a leadership team retreat. Her ESTJ Type (MBTI® preferences: Extraversion, Sensing, Thinking, Judging) fit well with what I saw in her. While she was more reflective and quiet than what might be considered typical for her type, she was certainly directed outwardly and energized by interacting with others.

Those Sensing Types ("S") that are brought into leadership often show aspects of Intuition ("N"), as did Jennifer. Her scores came out in the mid-zone on three of the S-N Facet dichotomies, showing her situational flexibility, and she was out-of-preference (on the side opposite the of the overall preference) with a "2" on "Imaginative," showing a slightly clearer leaning in that direction as opposed to the Sensing type's more typical "Realistic" Facet.

On the Thinking-Feeling dimension, she had two out-of-preference scores in the direction of Feeling on "Accommodating" and "Accepting." It wasn't uncommon in the hospital community to find T's with one or both of these scales reflecting these out-of-preference responses, and it seemed to fit with the work of caring for patients. The Tough-Tender scale came out as mid-zone.

Her core Operational Values – those that she engages daily to manage her life well—are Drive; Autonomy; Competency; Order; Accountability; Reason; and Knowledge. These are in service to her core long-term or Life Values: Happiness; Family; Self-Worth; Love; Health; Pleasure; and Achievement. It is important to note that her complete prioritization of values supports the story of her #1 operational value, Drive, by seeing where Wealth, Power, and Fame show up in Jennifer's Life values. While I often find these in the bottom seven of twenty-one, they appeared in her middle seven and were in service to the core life values noted.

Jennifer's FIRO-B® (needs) results showed what was important for her to express (the *Expressed* score) and what was important for her to get (the *Wanted* score). Her highest scores (ranking from 1, low, to 9, high) came out on the *Wanted* scales, with a 9 for *Inclusion*, a 7 for *Control* and a 9 for *Affection*. Her low *Expressed* scores rather surprised me for her Type and values. This gave me some hint that she might not be quite so secure and confident as I had thought, having little experience with her at this point. Now remembering the Accepting, Accommodating scores on the MBTI®, I felt there might be something more there than I thought initially.

Jennifer spoke easily about her life, even mentioning that she had been abused as a child and in her first marriage, experiences which had led her into some counseling. She was happy to report that she was now in a good, caring marriage and enjoyed life with her current husband and her daughter from her first marriage. It seemed that the counseling had been very beneficial and left her quite grounded and agile.

I enjoyed Jennifer's energy and involvement with the leadership work I did over the next couple of years with the Emergency department. She seemed happy, in control, and on track with her goals and interests.

Then one day, quite by accident, I heard that Jennifer was strongly considering leaving her position, and maybe even the hospital. I decided to reach out to her. I immediately began to think that something had happened that triggered some of the feelings of helplessness or shame with which victims of abuse are often left.

Jennifer was eager to get together, and I soon learned she was pretty resigned to the decision to leave her job, the hospital, and even her work as a doctor. I was now convinced that something did happen that was very unsettling for her psychic landscape.

After talking with her for at least an hour, I asked her not to make any quick decisions. She replied that she had to because her boss was waiting to hear what she was going to do. Knowing her boss, I assured her that I could get her more time and that we needed to at least explore whether this was the best decision and what her options were. The ground below her feet was obviously shaky, and she was quite sure the only option she had was to leave. Saki Santorelli says that when we're sick "we often take refuge in outer authority, forsaking our innate strength and healing capacity" (Santorelli 1999). Jennifer was certainly sick, or unwell, although more emotionally than physically. We needed to find some compensation for the one-sided response Jennifer was having; and to accomplish that, she needed to reconnect with her authentic Self. Her belief that the external environment wanted her to leave, that she wasn't good enough, was both a response to, and stimulation for, mounting anxiety.

What precipitated this shake-up was the loss of a patient. Someone who had come into the ED that she cared for and discharged died within 24 hours. She was devastated. And worst of all, she felt she could have done better. By the time we reconnected, Jennifer learned that she was being sued by the family for negligence.

Very quickly things were adding up. Jennifer agreed to some coaching if her boss would allow for it. Why lose such an important leader and employee if it isn't necessary? I soon learned that her boss was also devastated. He had been grooming her to be his successor and he wanted to know where he stood. The other senior leader in the department had been quite supportive of Jennifer, and I quickly spoke with both leaders to get their perspectives on the story and to enlist their aid.

With a commitment to a five-to-six- month coaching engagement and time secured for Jennifer to make a good decision about leaving or pulling out from the Chair succession, we got our work underway. There were a lot of feelings and emotions ping-ponging around in Jennifer's mind. We first wanted to settle the *angst* as much as possible, so that she could refrain from mental gymnastics and make good decisions for herself. Yes, she could leave…yes, there were surely other things she could do…yes, she could even take a break for a while and do something mindless. She told me that she found support from her daughter who she was sure is a "Feeling" Type—"She *forces* me to talk about my feelings." It was reassuring for me to know that she had that kind of relationship and support outside of our conversations.

Over the next six months, we looked at her options and focused on high points and low points in her work weeks. She was a bit resigned to doing something much less taxing and much more safe. When we reviewed her MBTI® Type and VAL® prioritized values list, she was surprised to realize that even if she took on something with less pressure and responsibility, it would be no time at all before she was in a leadership role again. She probably wasn't ready to "take it easy." She was also having good experiences with lots of positive feedback from staff because her team's metrics were strong.

During the time of our work, Jennifer and her family were looking for a new house and found one that bordered the water, which was something she really wanted. A new, tranquil environment can be very healing, and I felt her need to move to one *now* was potentially a metaphor for the work she had to do at the depths of her self. I encouraged her to pick up again a mentor-mentee relationship that she'd had with a senior leader in the department, and she agreed that would be a good idea.

I was aware of my own desire to connect Jennifer with more of her true Self. I wanted her to be able to see this as a part of the individuation journey that held real value for her. I was witnessing the out-of-balance wounded healer archetype so clearly and hoped she could find that inner healer for her old and new wounds.

While her boss was eager to know if she was staying or leaving, he, too, became more understanding about his role in the difficulty of the situation. While at first he felt betrayed, he came to see that he put a lot of pressure on her as the "good daughter": the "daughter" that affirmed his contribution and valued his knowledge and leadership. (He too was seeking balance for the wounded healer within.) He realized that he needed to separate her and himself from such expectations.

"Margin quote: Your journey has molded you for your greater good, and it was exactly what it needed to be. Don't think that you've lost time."

Asha Tyson

The imposter syndrome was an important topic of our work for several weeks. Jennifer felt this was a very real issue for her. This is a syndrome that afflicts women much more often than men. It is quite common. It had had some impact on her cognitively, but it was now also affecting her behaviorally and emotionally. She didn't trust herself in her physician role and noted she didn't "feel as smart clinically," and didn't "know as much as others."

Some noted that Jennifer was demanding perfection from everyone around her. One physician said that she called and *chastised* him for what she considered a lack of commitment. Others noted they found her to be intimidating. We talked about the idea of an "addiction to perfection" (drawing on Marian Woodman's work in a book of the same title). She felt she was her own worst critic. She noted that she was afraid to feel anything—anger, sadness, joy—and that she had never allowed herself such loss of control.

She was preparing to leave. She picked a successor. Perhaps one of her fears was being even more exposed if she stuck around. Then one day, she talked about her impatience and her realization that she had never given herself time to work through these kinds of issues. She added that she was finding our work very helpful. She closed on her new house, which gave her a positive activity upon which to focus her attention. She was also visiting colleges with her daughter and prepping for a triathlon at this time. Regarding the ESTJ Type, there was no doubt that "drive" *was* important. She told me "the running hurts so bad that it requires all of my thought and doesn't allow for much ruminating." My thought: *You need a new pastime!* But truly, I was impressed. (Relative to the transference/counter-transference, I think she *needed* to impress me, and potentially others, as she was feeling so impotent in her work.) By the way, she came in second in her age group.

We prepped for a one-to-one with her boss. Jennifer was eager to clear the air between them and come to some common understanding. He's an INTJ (Introverted, iNtuitive, Thinking, Judging in MBTI® Typology) and competence is quite important. He has an inward focus and she an outward focus. We talked about mutual respect and honest listening to value the experience of the other and rebuild trust. The two did have some core values in common, and we discussed how *Knowledge, Competency,* and *Autonomy* in their top operational values played into the conundrum. Their core life values were even more similar with 5 out of 7 the same: *Happiness, Family, Self-Worth, Health, and Pleasure.* This gave us a lot to work with in considering how they aligned and in identifying their sticking points.

The meeting went well and brought Jennifer some relief, enabling her to breathe better. Her boss confessed that he could be a bulldozer and not listen well. She shared that when she feels uncomfortable she doesn't communicate well. Following this meeting she was feeling "more settled" and "at peace with things." She said she felt more understanding of his initial annoyance and that a sense of justice had been restored a bit for her.

> "I must be willing to give up what I am in order to become what I will be."
>
> ALBERT EINSTEIN

What became clear over time was that Jennifer no longer wanted to be Chair. The role was so compelling for so many years that she now felt stuck in the expectation that she would be the one to fill it. Her boss had been grooming her—providing opportunities to stretch herself and develop her leadership. This was uncomfortable for her, and leaving because of the incident would have put an end to it. But she was now entertaining the idea that she might not want to leave; she might want to simply adjust her focus. She was moving out of a fragile state and finding her strength again. She was beginning to consider whom she could mentor and how she could help the department replace her as Associate Chair. Things were still ambiguous for her and that's not a place where she liked to live…but I encouraged her to move through it slowly. Santorelli reminds us,

> For all of us, our willingness to explore our fears, to live inside helplessness, confusion, and uncertainty, is a powerful ally. Acknowledging our repeated exposure to human suffering—our own and others'—and the seductive draw of numbness or melancholy that provides temporary escape is necessary if we are to be renewed. Our losses, our sense of self-importance and staunch individuality, and our unacknowledged grief can all be worked with as a way of entering the deep, encountering ourselves more fully, reconnecting to our own humanity and, in turn to the humanity of those with whom we come in contact. This is the soldier's work, and it is our work as well. (Santorelli 1999)

Soldiering On

We were nearly three months into our work now, and I asked Jennifer where she was, mentally and emotionally, with the swampland she had been experiencing. She said she was "still confused" but had "more hope and energy." She realized she needed to be patient in spite of the fact that she much preferred clear five- and ten-year plans. I thought she sounded and looked more upbeat and engaged. She seemed ready to raise her leadership and not run away from it. I asked her what she could state now that she couldn't just two months ago. She replied, "I want to stay in medicine." I was relieved, as I had surmised that this was the case, although I was aware of the projection. She added that she was enjoying her clinical practice again. Wow, that was a big change. She was also enjoying the administrative side of her work and feeling as if she were more attuned to her strengths and weaknesses. She was leading again, all of her actions were lining up with her words, and she was adjusting well.

In December, now four months into our work, Jennifer was starting to express the need for more clarity in the role she would play. She had ideas and energy and wanted to get more directed again. I discussed an idea with her called *The Bigger Game*™. This was a way to reconnect her with meaning-making in her life—to identify what was really calling her. The approach has nine elements built in to support the development of a successful strategy. It starts with creating a compelling purpose. We talked about the importance of staying tethered to the ideas that were forming in her as really important ones and discussed next steps for finding allies that would support her.

> "We don't so much solve our problems as we outgrow them. We add capacities and experiences that eventually make us bigger than the problems."
>
> C.G. JUNG

As time went on and Jennifer began to define her new life and work with hard-won confidence and authority, she needed less support and we got together less often. She renewed relations with her internal office mentors and inner *board of directors*. I had been growing and learning too, and I had to prepare myself for a new way of being in the world as well. Most people wouldn't have noticed this, but I knew it. When Jennifer and I connected on this part of her journey, she was feeling weighed down and in need of some guidance. My nature is to support those in need. So, in a way, her need was meeting my need. I was feeling buoyed up by the opportunity to support her. Now that our work was coming to an end and Jennifer was finding her stride, her needs diminished and I fell to the background. While I was delighted for her, I couldn't help but feel a little brushed aside. But this is often how the work of the coach, and others in the caring/supporting professions, goes.

In a poem called *Sunset*, Rainer Maria Rilke wrote:

...leaving you (it is impossible to untangle the threads)
your own life, timid and standing high and growing,
so that, sometimes blocked in, sometimes reaching out,
one moment your life is a stone in you, and the next, a star.
(Housden 2004)

I believe that both Jennifer and I were experiencing these alternating moments of feeling as if a stone were weighing us down on the inside and of feeling like a rising star. Sometimes our emotions were similar and sometimes they were in opposition, by the very nature of what we were gaining or losing in our position in the relationship and in our worlds. As I was observing her growth and disentangling her needs and hopes from my own, something loosened within me. As I noted needless worry or concern in me, the weights released, giving way to a new lightness.

In his writing about Rilke's poem, Roger Housden notes, "(it) captures in perfect pitch the essence of what it means, and also what it feels like, to be truly human."

Jennifer and I met in a very human place, both of us with real human needs—feeling despair and loss, hope and possibility, along with countless other emotions playing out along the way.

Jennifer's story is about the time she spent in a crucible; a time when things heated up and she melted down. In his book on resilience, Thomas notes,

> The journey that transforms an individual into a leader is often a lonely one. We only truly know one side of any conversation: our own. We know every torturous turn and pang of our own ordeals and rites of passage, but we never know more than a cartoon version of anyone else's. Unable to hear another's interior monologue, you may not realize that he or she is struggling at all. (Thomas 2008)

In the time of alchemical practice, metals were put into crucibles to be melted down into a liquid in an effort to create something new, more valuable. Alchemists were most commonly looking to change base metals into gold. The crucible experience for a person is a critical testing and defining period. Putting a twist on a common metaphor, I'd say Jennifer's "metal was being tested." She did come out of the experience as something new—something stronger and wiser. And so did I.

Returning to the wisdom of Saki Santorelli: "Perhaps our real work, whether offering or seeking care, is to recognize that the healing relationship—the field upon which patient and practitioner meet—is, to use the words of the mythologist Joseph Campbell, a 'self-mirroring mystery'—the embodiment of a singular human activity that raises essential questions about Self, Other, and what it means to *heal thy self*"(Santorelli 1999).

When I met with Jennifer a year later and two years later, I could see she was forgetting, little by little, the torment of those days when she was in the crucible. By the time I went to her to ask if I could use her story in this book, I was sure much of what we went through was a distant memory. She was strong and confident and excited about her work and her many contributions since that difficult time. I was reminded how Jung noted so beautifully that "…the path is a very powerful thing; as soon as you move upon it, it is no longer as if you were led by a guide, or guiding yourself, it is as if the path itself took command" (Douglas 1997). The path took over in our work together and picked right up where our work ended—she on hers and I on mine. This is how we individuate. We both had to reclaim our wholeness as we built up our capacity to go on about our lives as wounded healers.

> "The privilege of a lifetime is to become who you truly are."
>
> C.G. JUNG

Jennifer's Thoughts in Reflecting on This Period of Her Life

I thought I was pretty hard-core. I prided myself on being tough and thought I could handle anything life, and my career, threw at me. But this experience was something I was wholly unprepared for. What happened engendered such intense shame and isolation and threatened the core of my identity as a physician, and, therefore, as a person. Usually quite decisive, I began second-guessing my clinical decisions, and then some larger decisions, like my specialty choice and even my value as a physician. It was an extremely painful time for me, probably the darkest period of my life (easily overshadowing the difficulties of my earlier divorce and subsequent years as a single parent in medical school). I saw no way out of the pain, other than drastic options like quitting medicine entirely.

The healing process was long and not easy. Understanding why I had such an intense reaction, and having my experience and my feelings normalized (no, I wasn't crazy or weak or stupid) was a huge help. With time, I was finally able to rediscover my confidence and some of the aspects of medicine that brought me joy. Once I was able to share my "story" with others, I truly understood that I was not alone and that it was important for me to continue to talk about it so that others in similar situations would not feel isolated. Working to change our medical culture and to create an environment that is supportive of "second victims" continues to be a source of growth and healing for me.

"Jennifer"

Your Notes

What has become clear for you through this example? What are you feeling right now? What are you thinking? How will you make use of these feelings and thoughts?

IV

Asking Ourselves Questions on the Path to Growth and Effectiveness

God will not look you over for medals,
degrees or diplomas, but for scars.

Elbert Hubbard

Coaches often perfect the questions they ask of others, but rarely do I find that we spend any considerable time on the questions we ask ourselves. Of course, it's easier to enter the dark, tight places of others than it is to enter our own…and why complicate things? If you've read the earlier chapters, you know well how projection is useful, and how when it remains unconscious it can be harmful or, at best, negate the opportunity for serendipitous insights. Being blind to your own psychology sets you up for self-aggrandizement and charlatan behaviors. It follows that taking time to pause to ask yourself good questions can increase energy and creativity, strengthen your concentration, and enhance your ability to move forward with a client as well as to heal yourself. Good questions are the keys that open doors.

Catalytic Questions

In one of my Jung seminar sessions at the Philadelphia Association of Jungian Analysts, our instructor introduced us to a list of questions he has been working with over the years. He refers to these questions when he finds himself stuck in a session or in reflection after a session. The original material came from Mel Marshak, Jungian analyst and author, and I have adjusted it for coaches.

We'll start with some good basics. These are questions you might give cursory consideration to in the moments between meetings, and then reflect on more deeply as soon as you can make time.

- What expectations do I have for this engagement? For this client?
- How did I feel when I was with this client?
- How is this client affecting me?
- What is occurring between me and this client?
- What keeps me from saying what I want to say or need to say?
- What keeps me from sitting still and being silent?

Remember these are questions you are asking of yourself, drawing upon the catalyst within. You might want to pause now and make some notes on any that strike a chord for you at this time. Once you've reflected on these questions as they relate to a few of your current clients, think about how you might ask them regularly. Observe over time the resultant changes.

The first time I asked myself, "What is keeping me from saying what I want?" I was shocked to realize that there actually was something I was holding back. I was unaware of feeling intimidated by a particular leader, yet upon further reflection, there it was. I had buried that feeling in my impatience with what I perceived as arrogance. Once it came to light, I was able to work through my own inhibitions (bringing a bit of my own arrogance into play) and do much better work with my client. I actually came to enjoy our meetings, drawing greater agility from myself, and I'm quite sure my client found them more attuned to his style and, as a result, more useful.

Sometimes you are well aware of discomfort during a session, whether you just aren't feeling focused or you lack connection with the client. Here are some questions that can help you uncover the cause:

- How and where am I blocked with this client?
- What is going on inside of me when there is a blockage or an issue?
- How is my coaching activity moving the process forward or maintaining the status quo?

This last question has helped me on several occasions. On one particular occasion, I felt obliged to stay with a client, but at the same time I was feeling bored with the lack of movement. In each session, she retold the same stories she had told in previous sessions. I decided to try being more directive rather than remain a patient listener. I started by summarizing some of what I got from her stories and then asked, "So where do we go from here?" She replied, "I'm really not sure...I'm so surprised these stories lay dormant inside of me for so many years. What will I do with them?" Well of course that re-energized and re-focused the conversation.

Sometimes you have a feeling that the client is manipulating or derailing the coaching session. Questions that might be useful in these situations include:

- How is the client utilizing me?
- What are the client's expectations that "force" or "prod" me into a certain role, mold, or particular way of being with them?
- What am I doing to the client that "prods" them or "forces" them into a certain way of being with me?
- What lies behind or between the client's words?
- What does my imagination or my reverie tell me about the client?
- By what means has this client survived?

This last question might stimulate you to ask the following questions of yourself:

- By what means do I survive?
- Are there similarities? Differences?
- Do I have judgments on the way s/he is surviving in a different way from how I survive?

In a recent meeting, a client noted how she has difficulty with people who are not as practical and hardworking as she is. I realized that she has survived by being focused and tenacious. She's about to be promoted to a very senior role and this approach alone will no longer suffice. It shed some light on my needing to bring this to her attention and explore her capacity for developing greater range in her leadership style.

71

As you intentionally reflect on what might be unconscious in you that needs or wants to be made conscious, consider these questions:

- What symbols or images come to my mind to describe the process with this client? *(You might sketch those images.)*

- Which aspects of this client and session make me come alive? Which ones make me go dead?

- Am I afraid of disappointing or hurting this client? Why do I feel this way?

- How do I create reflective space in and around the session for both the client and me?

- Am I having any fun in our sessions, or are they only hard work?

- Does the language I use reflect my voice, or does it reflect more of a textbook voice?

- What goes on in my body during the session with this client?

- What do I do to be seen as an "ideal" person/coach, in order to avoid carrying "shadow"?

- How am I taking care of myself in the session with this client?

- What takes away my ability to function effectively?

- If the engagement doesn't go well can I learn from it and be okay with it, versus blaming my client or beating myself up?

As you read and considered all of these questions, did other questions come to mind? What will it take to commit to this type of reflection?

In an Executive Coaching professional group that I lead, I asked the group to review these questions and to pick one or two that they found interesting and to try using them as part of a reflection after their client meetings. They came to the next meeting quite enthusiastic about the experience. Here are some of their thoughts:

> I like the question, "How do you feel when you're with this client?" because I haven't always been tuned into my emotional state in a work setting when I am directly connected to the other person with whom I'm interacting. I've now learned and accepted that

my emotions and even my physical state—before, during, and after interacting with others—convey important meaning and enable me to provide more effective coaching.

I now regularly reflect on the question, "How do I feel when I'm with this client?" because I value the deep insights my feelings give me. There was a particular coaching relationship through which I learned my empathic capability was a door into understanding what my client was experiencing, as well as a perfect way for me to help her explore and wrestle with what would most help her on the leadership journey.

Reflecting on my feelings gives me an opportunity to sort out what is mine from what is "theirs," and then use what is theirs to spark learning and growth. At the same time I am continuously learning and growing.

Gina Gibbons, Pharma HR Leader

Another participant, who has spent many years in HR, Talent Management, and coaching, was drawn to the question, "How do I create reflective space in and around the session for both myself and the client?"

I have long supported the value of the MBTI® assessment. As a very clear Extravert, I have found this question useful in reminding me of the importance of reflection both during and between meetings with my client. This client is also an Extravert and quiet reflection is not a natural state.

I have used the "lesson" of this question to build in reflective questions during our meetings—to pause and reflect re: what has been useful, what is meeting his needs, and/or what else might add to the value of the session.

In addition, the client has found it useful to "schedule" time to reflect on his longer-term goals—this space has been reserved to focus his energy on his passion/desires for his future, above the immediate response he is having to his daily and weekly activity. This reflective space is occurring outside of our time together and, to date, has added to his ability to move closer to his ideal.

As I prepare for the next meeting with this client, I am also pausing, giving myself space to reflect on our work. I'm taking time to consider what is appearing to provide the greatest value, what might be getting in the way, and what I might do to move closer to my own version of success—the definition provided by the client and refined by the client during our interactions—and to prepare questions for reflection as we meet again.

Fredy-Jo Grafman, Principal, Unleash Talent & Gain Results

Another colleague relayed this story:

"What keeps me from saying what I want to say or need to say?" is a question I used after a coaching session with an executive client who had a pattern of explosive outbursts. He would "soldier on" despite conditions where others' performance was not up to his standard, or he felt the request for work was unfair. He often came off to others as a know-it-all. He fully understood the outbursts were detrimental on many levels, and we were working on increasing his awareness leading up to such incidences and finding more appropriate tactics to address what challenged him.

In a particular meeting, he was explaining his actions in a recent incident with his boss. After fifteen minutes or so, I interceded with a couple of questions. He talked over me and did not respond. I held off, which was a good move. However, I wanted to come back into the conversation and have him reflect on his behavior during our meeting— to use it as an example of stoking his own fire and not being able to hear the other person—but I did not.

Using this question helped me recognize that I did not want to feel diminished by my client or get fired by him. My own fear had held me back from providing a potentially powerful, in real time, example. In the subsequent meetings, I overcame my concerns and provided my questions, which led to great insights for the client.

Wendy Axelrod, Ph.D., Executive Coach, Author and Speaker

Yet another colleague asking the same question, "What keeps me from saying what I want to say or need to say?" shared this outcome:

About half way through a nine-month coaching engagement, I saw a noticeable difference in my client and felt she was not fully engaged and no longer committed to coaching. In fact, in my self-reflection notes after our session I made a note: "Ask her to be honest and tell me if she is still invested in the work and committed to continuing."

Instead of following my intuition, I tried finding other approaches to further challenge her. I refrained from telling her that I sensed she wasn't fully invested or committed to coaching. What kept me from saying this? Was she not ready to hear this yet? Or was I letting my ego get in the way? Was I afraid of what she might say? Was I afraid of being rejected? For years, I've tried to look inwards first if things aren't going well—was I being too hard on myself? Did I think her lack of engagement was somehow my fault or wouldn't have occurred if I used other approaches? Although creating new approaches provided me with some great coaching material, this wasn't where I needed to place my focus—it wasn't getting to the heart of the matter—for her growth or for mine. Ironically, in a wrap-up meeting, her manager disclosed that from the beginning she wasn't a good candidate for coaching. So perhaps it wouldn't have mattered after all if I had told her what I had wanted to say. However, having the opportunity to reflect on this question helped me realize how critical intuition is for successful coaching. Whenever I stray from using my intuition, I miss opportunities for growth and development. Having a self-reflection practice after client sessions has been invaluable for me. Incorporating these self-reflection questions in this practice has helped challenge me as a coach to stay objective, to get below the surface, to test the waters, and act upon those intuitions—which I believe contain the true golden nuggets for my success.

Marlene Carol Harding
Executive Coach, Leadership and OD Consultant
Principal, Inside Out Solutions, LLC

These fears of diminishment, intimidation, being wrong, and getting fired are the ego's response. Once the ego can access the Self, we arrive in a better place. Fear lies at the root of most of our problems. If we're alert to the fear we can use it to our benefit. James Hollis, speaker, analyst, and author, speaks of fear of abandonment and fear of being overwhelmed as fundamental to human activity. Fear grips us. It is often restrictive, driving us into deep, tight, and often painful places. Welcome to the ego's world. To release ourselves and come to our true nature—our authentic way—we must get below the fear and bring what is more real to consciousness.

A final important question we must ask ourselves as new opportunities arise is: do I have the bandwidth to take on another client at this time? While it is hard (fearful for the ego) to say no to new work, it doesn't serve us to be overextended. Being so overwhelmed is likely to draw out the charlatan or the narcissist within us, bringing on inauthenticity and uncomfortable outcomes. After one such experience, a coach colleague, whom I'll call Jonathan, said, "I crashed and burned for 3 months and then it took another 3 months to re-collect myself and then re-establish my business." While you might think this is a terrible outcome, and indeed, it was a difficult situation to endure at first, it was actually very useful to the rest of his career. Jonathan became much more mindful of his own capacity and what he really wanted for himself and his work/life experience.

Integration of the Insights

Our commitment to asking the questions, to reflecting on our responses, to being vulnerable, brings us valuable insights and enables our growth. In talking about this expansion of a person, Jung said,

> To establish a really mature attitude, he has to see the subjective value of all these images which seem to create trouble for him. He has to assimilate them into his own psychology; he has to find out in what way they are part of himself; how he attributes for instance a positive value to an object, when as a matter of fact it is he who could and should develop this value. And in the same way, when he projects negative qualities and therefore hates and

loathes the object, he has to discover that he is projecting his own inferior side, his shadow, as it were, because he prefers to have an optimistic and one-sided image of himself. (Jaffé 1989)

When we begin to do this reflective work it is important to know that we will not be the same. One of the analysts that worked closely with Jung, Marie-Louise von Franz, noted that, "any withdrawal of a projection lays a burden on the reflecting person. He becomes responsible for a piece of his psyche that he has hitherto regarded in an unburdened fashion as not being part of him" (Franz 2001).

So, you may ask, if this reflective work and seeing the darker aspects of myself encumbers me in new ways, why would I do this work? *To add more meaning and depth to my life* would be my main answer. Because for a while you will be happy with your income, your opportunities, but soon, something else, something deeper will need to be satisfied. The Self will be knocking at your door, drawing your attention inward, asking you to unlock the treasure trove of abundance waiting for you there. We do this work so that we can know and honor the true Self. Secondarily, it enables us to become much more effective in our work with others.

It is critical to remember that we do this work without judgment. This is about growing up, it's about expansion; it is not about right or wrong.

Writing Follows the Asking

It is hard to do this work on our own, maybe even impossible. Working with an analyst or a therapist has been very useful to me on this journey. Other approaches I have found to help unburden me include working with dreams, poetry, and writing.

Writing is healing. Journaling and taking time to write down our feelings provides a release and yet is a container. It is a way to further tap into our unconscious and see our complexes more clearly—to see where we feel inadequate, inferior, unprepared to show up—to come face-to-face with the shadow. If we only answer those questions in our minds we lose the ability to really grasp the full insight. Shadow is elusive. Our ego wants to keep us protected. But what we uncover when writing is available for us to come back to and work with when we're ready. We can then unleash our insights on a homeward journey toward psychological wholeness. A whole personality is a more aware and more comprehensive one. It is more emotionally stable. We can go from fragile to agile…with our selves, our families, and our clients.

Professor and author James W. Pennebaker, Ph.D. has provided illuminating research about expressive writing. He found that much of our physical and mental health and work performance improves from writing exercises. He suggests writing about, "something that you are thinking about or worrying about too much; something that you are dreaming about; something that you feel is affecting your life in an unhealthy way; or something that you have been avoiding for days, weeks, or years" (Pennebaker 2017). He says we should write about our *deepest emotions and thoughts*, or *most upsetting experiences*, and write merely for ourselves. I agree with his directive of really letting go (set the ego aside) and tying your thoughts to childhood experiences, parental or other relationships, or your work. Plan to burn what you write, erase it, tear it up, or get rid of it in some ritual manner; if you write with the idea of destroying it you can be more honest.

Patrick Kavanaugh begins his poem "The Self Slaved" with, "Me I will throw away, me sufficient for the day, the sticky self that clings adhesions on the wings to love and adventure." What a great line. When it pops into my head, unbidden as I go about my life, I know there's a little morsel of unconsciousness finding its way to the surface, seeking my attention. *Enough, enough,* it seems to be saying. *Stop the persona activity and find your true self.*

Writing (journaling) in response to the questions we ask can help us make a descent and enable us to re-emerge stronger, more satisfied. Dropping judgment in the process helps to unearth insights that impact our health and our lives in very positive ways. Being able to see life from a "both/and," non-dualistic perspective, even in short spurts, can re-enliven our spirit.

Your Notes

How have you been impacted by this chapter? What do you want to do as a result? Which of the questions are most powerful for you?

V

The Transformation of Organizations

A group experience takes place on a lower level of consciousness than the experience of an individual. This is due to the fact that, when many people gather together to share one common emotion, the total psyche emerging from the group is below the level of the individual psyche. If it is a very large group, the collective psyche will be more like the psyche of an animal, which is the reason why the ethical attitude of large organizations is always doubtful. The psychology of a large crowd inevitably sinks to the level of mob psychology. If, therefore, I have a so-called collective experience as a member of a group, it takes place on a lower level of consciousness than if I had the experience by myself alone.

C.G. JUNG,
*The Archetypes and the
Collective Unconscious* (CW #9)

So far, we've been focused primarily on our personal wounded healer experience and how it has an impact upon our work with our clients. We have reflected on how the wounded healer across from us in a coaching session may have an entirely different perspective because of how his experiences have shaped him. We know our reactions often flow from our woundedness and that we project onto one another in our discourse. But how (and why) might we consider the wounded healer at a collective level, where we focus on the organization and the many, as opposed to the individual?

The Evolution of Collective Wounding

At the individual level, we aim to differentiate ourselves from the other; at the collective level, we are sameness—all employees of "X" organization, working with line-of-sight toward a set of overarching goals. Organizations develop corporate values to encourage all to behave in like ways—according to their "core values." Clear expectations create *alignment* and people who *fit* the corporate culture. Taken to an extreme, alignment to these values and culture can wound people—cutting them down to size or stretching them unmercifully to meet the dimensions of a Procrustean bed. But managed well, alignment encourages positive behaviors and standards for cordial dynamics within the organization and customer relationships.

Does it change things for our work if we are working in an organization where there have been difficulties? For instance, what is the projected woundedness of an organization that recently lost a beloved leader to illness or accident? What were the projected wounds of the financial services organizations that *did* survive the financial crises in 2009? How would you imagine that woundedness to be different from that of the financial services organizations that suffered the loss of many colleagues in 9/11? And how would reactions be different for those who were there on the WTC site and survived, versus their co-workers at another US site or in another country?

Our work as executive coaches is work within a system, within another system, and so on. For example, I might work with an accountant in the accounting department of a large organization with global reach that is affected by several geopolitical environments. Without getting too complex, what does it mean to the coach and the work when any aspect of the system goes through difficulty, disruption, trauma—downsizing, rightsizing, transformation, budget cuts, mergers, divestiture? All of these experiences impact the culture and the mythology of the entire organization. Having a meaningful mission and set of core values can help leaders respond well in such situations.

But what if the corporate culture is about power and greed versus care and protection? I worked for one organization whose mission was "wealth-building and wealth-protecting" and another whose was "caring for our neighbors...". What might be the projected energy, expectation, and needs from all of these different scenarios? Born from what wounds? And does it matter to you, the coach, and to your work with your client?

My experience says it matters a lot. In fact, I would go so far as to say that I am of little use to my client if I don't pay attention to this information. Over the years, whether working internally or as an external consultant, I garnered much information that provided me sufficient evidence of the value of learning about the wounds, pressures, and subcultures of an organization. For example, in one organization where I worked for five years in HR, the employees watched as one after another of the senior leaders "drank the Kool-aid" and bought into a particularly manipulative approach to leadership. People would use that exact expression with disgust and utter frustration, not sure what to do or how to stop the momentum.

In another situation, I was enjoying the energetic, inclusive culture of one organization I supported for several years, when the wheels came off the proverbial bus. A new president took over and proclaimed that the organization had been too relationship-focused and had to become performance-focused instead. I knew this organization to be both relational and accomplishment-driven through the leadership groups that I led, and I was surprised to hear of such a dictate in this contemporary corporate climate. He quickly made the changes that he felt necessary to achieve his goal, and, like air being let out of a tire, the joy mysteriously seeped out of each team and project. Within a year people had gone from loving the company and enjoying their work to having the Sunday blues—dreading coming to work on Monday morning.

A final example includes an organization that I worked in that appeared to have a contingent of about eight leaders that were considered the geniuses— placed high on a pedestal above all of the other employees, who were mere worker bees. How might you think this impacted the commitment of such worker bees? How could this influence one of the "geniuses" that you are contracted to coach? What is the wound such an organization suffers from? Trust, inflation, power, narcissism?

A highly publicized, noteworthy example was when GE proclaimed it would be Number One or Two in every field in which it competed. Along with seeing this as a a significant change, generating immense pressure, I couldn't help but wonder if they were committing every employee to over-identification with power and inflation and, with that commitment, creating a culture of aggressive competition that would influence many other practices and behaviors. In fact, one *Fortune* article explained the "rank and yank" system of GE's performance management that resulted in "losers" and "failures." It instilled an uncomfortable competition between employees, noting, "those workers who ended up on the wrong side of the ranking curve were penalized, usually by a denial of merit raises or bonuses, and sometimes by losing their job" (Olson 2013).

What can you expect from the organizational *mythos* where a senior leader cleans up a long-term addiction and commits to AA...from one where a senior leader loses a child or a spouse...from one where a senior team refuses to act as a team...from one where a part of the organization gets sold off to another organization? In the latter situation, it will be quite different for those who go and those who are left behind. I experienced this first-hand with an organization where several of those who "made the cut" and were kept on suffered survivor's syndrome. Certainly our consciousness of organizational wounding as coaches matters. The more clearly and compassionately we see our wounds, the wounds of others, and yes, even those of the organizational systems in which we work, the more power we have over them.

Organizational Shadow

One senior leader I collaborated closely with supported my work with a variety of his mid-level leaders, but when it came to my request to work with a leader (we'll call her Sylvia) above and beyond those mid-level leaders, he tersely shut it down with a definitive "no." He said, "I have it covered, I'm mentoring her." I tried to offer her some support and even direction when opportunities arose because of the pain I had witnessed trickling down from her leadership. Sylvia was erratic and defensive, and her pejorative interactions left many a ghost in the corporate closets. Jung might call it *organizational shadow*. Over the months following her separation (she was eventually terminated), the ghosts were showing up like mad and the senior leader was exposed for his folly. He had never been able to manage her, and, rather than mentoring her, it appeared that he had merely protected her. The organization had been severely damaged and many individuals also suffered. One in particular (that eventually engaged me for coaching) had come to the organization just a couple of years before Sylvia left. He was smart, highly experienced, held several degrees, had good energy, and was an excellent manager. Hired into one job in which his multidisciplinary team members were not engaging or supportive was a disappointment. But he was quickly ushered into a new role. It was a bigger role and much more challenging in its complexity. But he was a good fit…maybe too good. Sylvia badgered him and taunted him, told him outright that he *wasn't* a good fit and she could provide a soft landing should he want to leave. It seemed that she was intimidated by his competence and capacity. As Jean Shinoda Bolen puts it: "This is the wounding shadow of authority that says, 'I know what your story is and I know its meaning, and it robs the person of the opportunity to discover this.'" (Cruz and Buser 2016)

My client stuck it out, but the ghosts in his own closet, his personal shadow, his *inner critic*, was relentless. It made him sound paranoid and unbalanced in conversations with those he thought were his allies. As soon as his new leader was on board, she was given a file (possibly an actual file, but certainly a metaphorical one) on him, and at the first opportunity she told him he was being separated from the organization. Fortunately, we had done a lot of groundwork together and he was as relieved as he was disappointed. But because of early family expectations, aggravated by the corporate culture, he felt "ashamed." "What had I done so wrong?" he asked. James Hollis helps us to understand: "Most insidiously, a complex has the power to usurp the ego, plunder ordinary consciousness in the moment, oblige us to look through the regressive lens of history, and therein respond to this new moment, this new situation in an old way" (Hollis 2013).

Later people were telling me the larger organizational climate was moving to blame and shame from one of pride and gratitude. I was left to wonder how many more "gotcha's" would surface.

"The more powerful you are, the more your actions will have an impact on people, the more responsible you are to act humbly. If you don't, your power will ruin you, and you will ruin the other."

POPE FRANCIS

One-Sidedness

From our conversations on the archetype of the wounded healer with our conscious connection to one pole or the other ("wounded" or "healer" or some point along the continuum) we have bumped up against one-sidedness. This is not a bad or wrong thing in itself—we all are one-sided about many things. Even Typology introduces us to our one-sidedness as Introverts or Extraverts. That being said, Type and archetype are dynamic and different experiences that will bring out *more* or *less* clarity of preference. Some situations in our lives can make for a "stuckness" that can be disabling. This is what happens when we get stuck in the healer aspect and don't realize our woundedness.

Just as a person can suffer from one-sidedness, an organization can as well. For example, imagine what happens to an organization that is all enthusiasm, with little reflection and concern? I experienced this with a team that wanted me to facilitate work on "strengths" with them. They completed assessments and we discussed each of their top five strengths. I tried to carefully introduce the importance of realizing that overused strengths become weaknesses. They sounded mildly interested, but moved me right along into positive psychology oblivion…"We're the best team;" "We always help one another out;" "We appreciate each other's differences;" "We're like a family." They nodded and smiled like Stepford Wives, but behind them lurked shadowy ghosts burdened with confusion and despair. I had learned that they talked about each other's foibles in the back hallways. Typically that talk was passive-aggressive, *i.e.,* "Don't you think Tom looks sad today? I think he's been sad for a long time;" "I feel so sorry for Mary. I don't think she understands what we're trying to do." In reality, it seemed as though all of their collective insecurities were tossed in the same pot and they chose not to see it. But one day this co-mingling of their narcissistic woundings, simmering just below the surface, would surely boil over, in spite of all of the organization's "strengths".

Similarly, a group that is negatively one-sided—full of doom and gloom, or skepticism—also struggles. I have seen the seeds of this in regulatory and compliance, legal, and accounting departments. Good leadership that is aware of the dangers of one-sidedness in these departments is particularly important for incorporating balanced perspectives that lead to healthy outcomes.

As we have noted, emotions and incidences that lie hidden in the shadow realm are dangerous. The shadow of a wounded leader will be an imposition to all whom s/he serves. All in the hierarchy, all who live under her/his authority, are very likely to be affected. The culture of an organization starts at the top and evolves to meet the dominant attitudes. When difficult personalities (*i.e.,* all the things we don't like about others, all of the approaches that oppose our ideal or just don't make sense to us) are relegated to the shadow realms, we put the hope for healthy employees and healthy organizations at risk. When we as coaches ignore this information—types of leadership, past and present, their impact, their following—we enable the proliferation of lies, sins of omission, and collective wounding.

The Two Sides of Narcissistic Leadership

All leaders are narcissistic to some degree. It would be hard not to be when you consider what it takes to be promoted to the top levels of organizations and institutions. Could you do it if you didn't have some unwavering belief in yourself and the ability to forget your mistakes? If you didn't enjoy the admiration and power to some degree, would it be worth it? If you weren't daring and edgy, could you make enough of a difference?

In our current world paradigm, we are hearing and experiencing "VUCA" (volatility, uncertainty, complexity, and ambiguity). This combination is not for the faint of heart. Many spend their days wondering when it will stop and hiding out in safe places that allow them to do their work and stay away from the mayhem. But, for the narcissist, VUCA is invigorating, enabling them to be larger-than-life figures that go valiantly into the dust storm with grandiose ideas and actions. "Productive narcissists are experts in their industries, but they go beyond it. They also pose critical questions. They want to learn everything about everything that affects the company and its products" (Maccoby 2004). "The most important trait that plays into the successful leadership of [Jeff] Bezos is his narcissism. It plays into his strengths and even some of his dark side…He is known to push his team with such high demand and intolerance of failure that Amazon has had [problems with] turnover and burnout. He also likes to be in control of where his ideas go and to be in the center of the action" (Baksh 2016). Fortunately, his desire to meet his customer's expectations, his technical skills, and conceptual abilities make him a true inspiration.

Another famous narcissistic leader, Steve Jobs, struggled with leadership, had few friends, and was known for publicly humiliating his employees. He too was ingenious, hard-driving, and very skilled. By many accounts, he was also unempathic. One successful R&D leader I worked with described his empathy as "zero, none, goose egg." "In fact, in times of radical change, lack of empathy can actually be a strength. A narcissist finds it easier than other personality types to buy and sell companies, to close and move facilities, and to lay off employees—decisions that inevitably make many people angry and sad. But narcissistic leaders typically have few regrets. As one CEO says, 'If I listened to my employees' needs and demands, they would eat me alive'" (Maccoby 2004).

By contrast, unproductive narcissists go blindly and unabashedly forward, ignoring their followers and insisting on more and more adulation and autonomy. These leaders are very sensitive to criticism and are uncomfortable with their own emotions, and, rather than act as teachers or mentors, they indoctrinate others and dominate at meetings. "The result for the organization is greater internal competitiveness at a time when everyone is already under as much pressure as they can possibly stand. Perhaps the main problem is that the narcissist's faults tend to become even more pronounced as he becomes more successful" (Maccoby 2004).

Think about leaders from your own experience that are unproductive narcissists and consider what resonates for you—relative to that leader, the organization s/he works for, and yourself in your relationship with the leader and/or the organization. What are some of the ways power is used, abused? How does it impact the system? What emotions are acted out and which ones are silenced?

Many books have been written about the challenges of narcissism and narcissistic leaders. One stemmed from the reflections of a number of Jungians on their experience of the 2016 U.S. Presidential campaign. Here are some excerpts from *A Clear and Present Danger,* edited by Leonard Cruz and Steven Buser, that emphasize the woundedness from which such narcissism springs and from which it is fed:

> "Leaders are uniquely susceptible to intoxicating and inflating forces that are projected onto them." (p. xi)

> "The Trump/antiTrump showdown has become a kind of cultural complex in which the major attraction is surprisingly not so much Trump himself as a person, but the national psychodrama playing itself out in the collective psyches of various groups in the country and their differing projections onto Trump, for which he is a perfect hook." (p. 29)

> "But it is not Trump's narcissism that captures my attention as much as the narcissistic injury at the level of the group Self that I hypothesize about those who are so captivated by him." (p. 38)

> "…there is a good fit between Trump's personal narcissism and the narcissism of our culture and the wounded collective Self of many Americans." (p.40)

> "Jungians recognize that large groups of people can be overtaken by archetypal energies. Possession by an archetype is capable of unleashing tremendous collective force. According to Jung, possession is a state of mind in which 'complexes take over the control of the total personality in place of the ego, at least temporarily, to such a degree that the free will of the ego is suspended.'" (p. 70)

> (Cruz and Buser 2016)

A narcissistic leader I worked with sucked the air out of a room so quickly that the other attendees jumped on email, sending texts and editing documents during his meetings as a lifeline and means of getting through the hour. They knew it was only essential that they nod every so often to feign agreement. While I felt their pain, I couldn't help but be frustrated by their lack of willingness to fight for more collaboration. I wondered if they were conscious of their resignation. I wondered if this verbose leader became a good excuse for overworked and overwhelmed employees to get some work done. One day I watched with great curiosity as a very competent and effective leader pushed his way into the one-way conversation. It was impressive to observe his maneuvers and tenacity. But I felt exhausted for him for all of the energy it took to get heard. Afterward I had to go about preparing for a debrief with my client (the narcissistic leader). I knew I would have to tread lightly and maintain his self-esteem in order to keep a trusted partnership. It was slow and tedious work. How was the collective at least partially responsible for his temporary success? Was it the result of too much busy-ness? Of apathy?

Staying Awake

When we look back at the communication table (Table 2, p. 32) and how we each, along with the organizations we work in, are expressing ourselves at conscious and unconscious levels (sometimes with quite different messages) all day long, we might wonder how we make any progress at all. When we remember from the discussion of the psyche (Table 1, p. 19) that we are more unconscious than conscious, are we additionally confounded by our successes?

> Large political and social organizations must not be ends in themselves, but merely temporary expedients...like cancerous growth, they eat away man's nature as soon as they become ends in themselves and attain autonomy. From that moment, they grow beyond man and escape his control; he becomes their victim and is sacrificed to the madness of an idea that knows no master.
>
> Jung, Collected Works 10, para. 219
> as found in (Corlett and Pearson 2003)

We must stay very intentional to maintain awareness of the autonomous complexes and *mythos* of an organization, in order to not lose control to them or become just another victim. In his poem "A Ritual to Read to Each Other," William Stafford writes,

For it is important that awake people be awake,

or a breaking line may discourage them back to sleep;

the signals we give—yes or no, or maybe—

should be clear: the darkness around us is deep.

Generational Connections to Narcissism

Millennials have been referred to as "the most narcissistic generation ever" (Brown 2017). In one NPR podcast, theirs was called "the age of the selfie" (Vedantam 2016). The reality is that narcissistic woundings show up in new ways in each new generation entering the workforce. Many Millennials were victims of an oversimplification of the self-esteem movement, where children were often mollycoddled and lavished with false praise. This movement backfired because developing false self-esteem was found to be of no benefit and often created emotionally fragile young adults.

A study of 15,000 papers on self-esteem showed that "having high self-esteem didn't improve grades or career achievement. It didn't even reduce alcohol usage. And it especially did not lower violence of any sort" (Mohler 2007). In the same article, Judith Brook, a New York University psychiatry professor, stated that credibility is paramount:

> "Praise is important, but not vacuous praise. It has to be based on a real thing–some skill or talent they have. Once children hear praise they interpret as meritless, they discount not just the insincere praise, but sincere praise as well" (Mohler 2007).

Organizations also have programs to affirm and celebrate individuals and teams for their skills and successes. Some are better than others, but they often get political and miss the point. The value of the coaching relationship is that of balance—we support and challenge our clients, and we acknowledge (celebrate) their successes and debrief their disappointments. We help them see their heroic side and their shadow. We work with the pride and the shame, and when we're at our best we value (honor) both.

When is a Choice Not a Choice

Too often I find people in large organizational roles who have little freedom to make choices for their own good. They get "tapped" for this role or that project, and they are supposed to be grateful and ignore the considerable downside. It can be almost predatory in nature. In many cases these opportunities seem to be much more favorable for the organization and less so for the individual. While the organizations hunt down the "best and the brightest" and promote them and pay them well, often enough individuals are taken advantage of and not given a lot of consideration in co-creating their development and their work. We've all heard of "golden handcuffs"—sweet deals to keep you with a company that are tempting, but when accepted without careful thought can lead to disenfranchisement and added tension in the system.

Most of my clients have calendars that are exploding with meetings, often starting at 7:30 AM and going till 5:00 PM. In global roles, they start earlier and can extend into the night with phone meetings. There are meetings to plan for meetings and meetings to debrief meetings. There are project meetings and staff meetings all in an effort to become more collaborative, inclusive, and responsive.

The majority of work environments are victims of VUCA. We've all become well aware that change is a constant and that innovation is necessary, but we may have missed the piece about volatility, uncertainty, complexity, and ambiguity's all becoming the norm. We talk about disruptive change and rapid cycle management, innovation and transformation, but we haven't imagined the impact to the collective environment when all of these things are happening at once. Even with our Lean Six Sigma and HiPo agility programs we can't keep up this pace. Thinking we can is *hubris*. How do we slow it down? Who gets to decide that it's just too much? Is it any wonder that when leaders are successful they often become highly inflated? How can we as coaches have an impact on pomposity? Will education in emotional intelligence and emotional agility be enough? How can we facilitate insights stemming from the psychosocial dance we all take part in at the individual and collective level?

The Gift of Consciousness

Many of our early feeling experiences are what constellate our shadow… and also get parsed into that big collective shadow of our companies and our country. Then we go about the unconscious business of transferring our resistance, our compliance, and our avoidance on to one another. We transfer our anger, our aggression, and our disappointments, too. We can recognize the narcissistic wounding that shows up in our personalities (or those of others) as the damage to our self-worth early in our lives. We might appear needy or have an addiction as adults. We try at all costs to have a cool veneer that says, I'm strong, I'm capable, and I'm committed. But underneath there lies another story. If the woundings are intolerable, they are buried deep and narcissists often evolve. Nancy Swift Furlotti, Ph.D., a Jungian analyst, says:

> The weak, insecure ego is always at great risk of being overwhelmed by the destructive forces of the unconscious. Instead, these forces are frequently discharged outward onto other people, groups, or objects. The narcissist's *persona* helps keep these forces in check to a small extent while in public, but the anger, envy, the need for control, and the grandiose exhibitionism that satisfies the ego's thirst for bolstering itself up by tearing others down, is ever-present. The shadow of wild, uncontrollable emotions from the negative side of the Self cannot remain beneath the insufficient mask of any *persona* for very long. (Cruz and Buser 2016)

So why do we consider the organization as collective wounded healer? Because if coaches can help facilitate consciousness in the leaders we work with, enabling more of them to work out of both sides of the wounded healer archetype, those who initially were only in touch with their strength (*i.e.*, healer), and those who were more controlled by their weakness (*i.e.*, wounds)—could integrate the two (the "both/and"). In this way, they could develop a wise and thoughtful strength. They would be more in tune with how important their conscious action is to the cultures they're creating. If more coaches as well as leaders were attuned to the value of giving attention to both aspects of the archetype, our collective communities would stand a chance of better leadership, stronger teams and collaborations, and more engaged and fulfilled employees. Isn't this why organizations invest in coaches?

Our work is to stay curious about ourselves, others, *and* the collective. It is for us to do our own inner work so that we can meet our clients just where they are. It is our remit to provide useful guidance and potentially even ease leaders' burdens. It is from this paradigm that we can ask the most useful questions, elicit clarifications, educate, and be educated. In a poem titled, "The Gift," Denise Levertov writes:

> "Just when you seem to yourself
> nothing but a flimsy web
> of questions, you are given
> the questions of others to hold
> in the emptiness of your hands,
> songbird eggs that can still hatch
> if you keep them warm..."

> And she finishes by noting, "You are given the questions of others
> as if they were answers
> to all you ask. Yes, perhaps
> this gift is your answer."

Every time someone recognizes and takes responsibility for his/her unconscious stuff, it lightens the burden for the rest of the group. Coaching is a mutual gifting and in the end we hope the gifts make for better communities in which to work and live.

Your Notes

What questions are on your mind? What client questions have surfaced in your thoughts? What do you want to do with, or because of, these questions?

_____

_____

_____

_____

_____

_____

_____

_____

_____

_____

_____

_____

_____

_____

_____

_____

_____

_____

_____

_____

_____

_____

VI

In Closing: Finding Acceptance, Endurance, and Authenticity

Speaking of the psychotherapist, Jung says:
"He is not just working for this particular patient,
but for himself as well and his own soul, and in so doing
he is perhaps laying an infinitesimal grain in the scales of
humanity's soul. Small and invisible as the contribution
may be, it is yet an opus magnum."

EDWARD EDINGER,
The Creation of Consciousness

Some of us come to our individuation by aiding others in theirs, all the while getting glimpses of insight for our own growth and potential. Circumambulating our complexes and the resultant personality, we eventually come to accept who we are, scars and all.

Yet we all must learn that once we discover and work with our wounds, we don't have to be identified with them; they are just part of this individuation journey, this process that brings us to greater levels of consciousness. Jung said, "If the individuality is unconscious, there is no psychological individual, but merely a collective psychology of consciousness" (Jung 1971). As we reviewed in Chapter 5, it is easy for our clients to get drawn into the collective with all of its *musts, shoulds,* and alignments. One can fall into the great melting pot, which we all do at times. It can be fine in the short-term, providing an opportunity to coast or catch our breath, but we must become conscious of our Self again and differentiate based on what is moving within.

Individuation is a slippery concept. We each get drawn into the striving our ambiguous and complex lives seem to draw us toward—striving to make enough money for all of the things we need, then striving for all of the things we want (or think we want). When we are striving we encounter all manner of obstacles. If we don't see and understand this in ourselves, we get drawn into our clients' striving, and we find ourselves entangled in merely helping them achieve the goals they think they must meet. Likely, these align with the goals of their bosses and HR leaders and are in service to their organizations' goals. They are goals that are important and useful, but attention to them alone takes people off their personal growth path. Jung noted that we must become conscious of our "peculiar nature." We spend so much of our lives wanting to be like others and not realizing the quest is to be our unique self.

Rilke writes (from "I Am Much Too Alone In This World, Yet Not Alone"):

I want to unfold
I don't want to stay folded anywhere,
because where I am folded, there I am a lie.

Unfolding can be scary—opening to the light of day takes courage—but it is necessary. And coaches who do their own unfolding are the best prepared to go down that path with others. Equipped with empathy and compassion from daring to look into our own woundedness and finding acceptance for who we are, we can support others in finding acceptance for who *they* are. And in our primed attentiveness, we can see and hear from them what is often not said, but only insinuated ever so briefly.

The poem goes on:
And I want my grasp of things
true before you. I want to describe myself
like a painting that I looked at closely for a long time.

We *do* look at ourselves for a long time—usually for 30, 40, 50 or more years—before we realize we are unique for a reason and have great value in our uniqueness. I used to be surprised at how honest clients would be about their fears and concerns. But now I realize how cleansing it is to find and tell our truth. Accepting ourselves for the long haul, not just a brief moment in time, requires tenacity and endurance. That can come with the circumambulation, reflection, and integration work we do for ourselves and that we support in others as coaches using an Analytical Framework (CAF, see appendix).

I realize over and over that our storytelling is every bit as important, if not more, than the aspirations and goals we express. Allowing others to share their stories, their truth, requires attentiveness, humility, and real caring that can only come from our doing our own work.

Our reflective work before, during, and after our sessions with our clients (return to the questions from chapter 4) enables these attributes to take hold in us along with the wisdom to know how to go forward. Staying in touch with difference and projection enlightens and educates us, so that the next step becomes apparent. But don't mistake diligence for striving for perfection. Perfection only minimizes our humanity and our ability to relate to others.

Additionally, a nice collaboration on the part of the organization (or the collective) and the individual allows for a good perspective on who we will or can become and who we really feel we're meant to be. That outcome often manifests not as what the individual initially brings to the table, and not what the sponsor brings, but some third thing—something new that transcends the conversation we started with.

> "To meet everything and everyone through stillness instead of mental noise is the greatest gift you can offer to the universe."
> ECKHART TOLLE

Reflecting on why we do what we do might be an alien concept. It might feel self-indulgent or unimportant, but I believe it is absolutely essential in this volatile, uncertain, complex, and ambiguous twenty-first century. We are experiencing new levels of disruption, disrespect, and neediness—me, me, me. We have so much, and yet we want so much more. All of the wanting masks what we really need. For what we really need is to value, respect, and love ourselves deeply enough, truly enough so that we can evolve. Like the caterpillar, we need to find a place to hang out, a safe place in which to molt into a chrysalis, transforming and emerging into a unique specimen.

The reflective work that we do enables our transformation: an expanded, unique perspective, for us, and in support of our clients. With this kind of devotion to the work, we have the ability to be the ship that Rilke describes at the conclusion of his poem:

...like a ship
that took me safely
through the wildest storm of all.

We're taken through our wildest storms by the support of others. And in turn, we support others through their wildest storms, so they may come out announcing who they are with real authenticity.

Mary Oliver concludes her poem "Wild Geese" (Chapter 1) by declaring

Whoever you are, no matter how lonely,
the world offers itself to your imagination,
calls to you like the wild geese, harsh and exciting-
over and over announcing your place
in the family of things.

We are never done...this work goes on and on. We don't find our confidence one day and check that box. We don't find our wounds, patch them up, and become healers. We are continuously called to integrate both aspects of this dynamic wounded healer archetype. We will find our self on many different points of the continuum in the course of our lifetimes. The world has a million ways to challenge us on this journey. Coaches who do their inner work will meet the challenges head-on. Remember Chiron, the wounded healer from Greek mythology? He seems to be conveying this important message to us in the twenty-first century: consciously seek your wholeness—seek your wholeness by taking lessons from daily life, walking

> "We are aided on our journey by inner guides, or archetypes, each of which exemplifies a way of being on the journey...Each has a lesson to teach us, and presides over a stage on the journey."
> CAROL PEARSON,
> *AWAKENING THE*
> *HEROES WITHIN*

the path with others, finding joy in your sorrows, staying curious, and listening attentively. In this way, we will live a truly authentic life and model authenticity for our clients.

Your Notes

What questions do you have as a result of completing this book? What do you want to do in the next week, month, year as a result of your questions and insights?

Other Suggested Reading

» *Depth Coaching: Discovering Archetypes for Empowerment, Growth, and Balance,* Patricia R. Adson

» *Power in the Helping Professions,* Adolf Guggenbühl-Craig

» *Psychological Types,* Collected Works #6, Carl G. Jung

» *The Fisher King & The Handless Maiden,* Robert A. Johnson

» *The Wounded Healer: Ministry in Contemporary Society,* Henri Nouwen

» *The Wounded Healer: Countertransference from a Jungian Perspective,* David Sedgwick

» *World Weary Women,* Cara Barker

References

Baksh, Dawn. 2016. "The builder, innovator and the narcissistic leader: Jeff Bezos." Penn State Liberal Arts Online, accessed May 28.

Brookes, I. 1994. "The death of Chiron: Ovid, Fasti 5.379-414." *The Classical Quarterly* 44 (2):444-450. doi: 10.1017/S0009838800043895.

Brown, Jessica. 2017. "Millenials are the most narcissistic generation ever." indy100, accessed 5/31. https://www.indy100.com/article/millennial-narchissistic-gen-y-narcissism-scale-study-7588141.

Cheung-Judge, Mee-Yan. 2001. "The Self as an Instrument - A cornerstone for the future of OD." *OD Practitioner* 33 (3):11-16.

Corlett, John G., and Carol S. Pearson. 2003. *Mapping the organizational psyche: A Jungian theory of organizational dynamics and change.* Gainesville, FL: Center for Applications of Psychological Type, Inc.

Cruz, Leonard, and Steven Buser, eds. 2016. *A clear and present danger: narcissism in the era of Donald Trump.* Asheville, NC: Chiron Publications.

Douglas, Claire, ed. 1997. *Visions: Notes of the seminar given in 1930-1934.* New (revised) ed. Princeton: Princeton University Press.

Edinger, Edward. 1984. *The creation of consciousness.* Canada: Inner City Books.

Franz, Marie-Louise von. 2001. *Psychotherapy.* Boston: Shambhala.

George, Bill, Peter Sims, Andrew McLean, and Diana Mayer. 2007. "Discovering Your Authentic Leadership." *Harvard Business Review.*

Guggenbuhl-Craig, Adolf. 1971. *Power in the helping professions.* Dallas, Texas: Spring Publications, Inc.

Hollis, James. 2013. *Hauntings: dispelling the ghosts that run our lives.* Asheville: Chiron.

Housden, Roger. 2004. *Ten poems to last a lifetime.* NY: Harmony Books.

Jaffé, Aniela, ed. 1989. *Memories, dreams, reflections.* Fourth ed. NY: Vintage Books. Original edition, Erinnerungen Traume Gedanken, 1961.

Jung, C. G. 1971. *Psychological types.* Translated by H. G. Baynes (with revision by R. F. C. Hull). Edited by executive editor William McGuire, Sir Herbert Read, M.D. Michael Fordham, M.R.C.P. and PH.D. Gerhard Adler. 18 vols. Vol. 6, *Bollingen Series XX.* Princeton: Princeton University Press.

Jung, C. G. 1989. *The symbolic life.* Translated by R. F. C. Hull. Edited by Herbert Read, Michael Fordham, Gerhard Adler and William McGuire, *Bollingen Series XX.* Princeton: Princeton University Press. Reprint, 3.

Langs, Robert, and Harold F. Searles. 1980. *Intrapsychic and Interpersonal Dimensions of Treatment.* New York Jason Aronson.

Levy, Paul. 2007. "The Wounded Healer." *my PTSD,* 5/6/17.

Maccoby, Michael. 2004. "Narcissistic Leaders: The incredible pros, the inevitable cons." *Harvard Business Review* 82 (1).

Mauger, Benig. 2013. "Chiron in the 21st century: Wounded healers today." Irish Association of Humanistic Integrative Psychotherapy, accessed 5/6/17.

Mohler, Albert. 2007. The self-esteem movement backfires: When praise is dangerous.

Olson, Elizabeth G. 2013. "Microsoft, GE, and the futility of ranking employees." *Fortune blogging*, 6/10/17.

Pennebaker, James W. 2017. "Writing and Health: Some practical advice." accessed April 20, 2017. liberalarts.utexas.edu/psychology/faculty/pennebak#writing-health.

Samuels, Andrew, Bani Shorter, and Fred Plaut. 1986. *A Critical Dictionary of Jungian Analysis*. London: Routledge, Taylor & Francis Group.

Santorelli, Saki. 1999. *Heal thy self: Lessons on mindfulness meditation*. NY: Bell Tower.

Sedgwick, David. 1994. *The wounded healer: countertransference from a Jungian perspective*. London: Routledge.

Thomas, Robert J. 2008. "Inside the crucible: learning and leading with resilience." In *Crucibles of leadership*. Boston: Harvard Business Press.

Vedantam, Shankar. 2016. Me, me, me: The rise of narcissism in the age of the selfie. In *Hidden Brain*, edited by Shankar Vedantam. NPR: NPR.

Wilder, A. Tappan, ed. 1997. *The Collected Short Plays of Thornton Wilder, Volume 2*. New York: Theatre Communications Group.

Appendix

Coaching with an Analytical Framework aligned with Jung's framework for analysis

ASPIRATION

Why do you want to engage in coaching? What are you wanting to do better, or be more effective at? What are your personal goals? Professional goals? What is your purpose? What does your manager think? What does HR think? Have you had a 360° assessment and what does it suggest? What do you aspire to? How have your aspirations led you to where you are today? Aspirations vs. inspirations? Rules of engagement (ie: confidentiality).

ASSESSMENT

Gather data through assessments; analyze and review with client; finalize development plans and connect with client sponsor. Assessment provides an opportunity for clarification and insight on "you" and a language for expressing yourself more fully. While most clients know themselves to some degree, much of the real insight has not been brought to light; elucidation is necessary where the point of fixation arises.

COACHING

Sessions with client where support and challenge are utilized to develop new skills and insights. Rapport is continuously developed through listening and clarification. We challenge the client to see the situation more clearly and ask questions from our own insights. Updates with manager or HR are intermittent as requested or appropriate. Plans are modified to enable the best outcomes.

TRANSITION

Closing out the process with the client in order to transfer them back to the full support of the system – manager, HR, and stakeholders. This is a time for celebration. New habits have been formed, new perspectives and attitudes adopted and a more resilient leader is ready to get back to the business of leading in a fully focused and confident way. However, not without a plan for continuing their development and ongoing insights in some thoughtful way.

CONFESSION

Recounting the truth of the moment; getting it out – giving voice to issues, concerns, realities. The act of having some trusted other hear your realities. Abreaction (Wikipedia 1/20/12) is a psychoanalytical term for reliving an experience in order to purge it of its emotional excesses; a type of catharsis. Sometimes it is a method of becoming conscious of repressed traumatic events.

ELUCIDATION

"While the cathartic method restores to the ego such contents as are capable of becoming conscious and should normally be components of the conscious mind, the process of clearing up the transference brings to light contents which are hardly ever capable of becoming conscious in that form. This is the cardinal distinction between the stage of confession and the stage of elucidation."

EDUCATION

New habits are won because of exercise and this requires education. "The patient must be drawn out of himself into other paths, which is the true meaning of education, and this can only be achieved by an educative will." The analyst may share a variety of thoughts and ideas allowing the patient to stretch, challenge and enlarge their world.

TRANSFORMATION

The doctor–patient relationship is very important to the outcomes. "For two personalities to meet is like mixing two different chemical substances: if there is any combination at all, both are transformed." The analyst must be open to influence in order to have influence in the analytic relationship. With this mutuality insights occur for both parties and they are transformed by the experience.

Steinwedel's CAF model/process

Jung's analysis model/process

Index

About Janet S. Steinwedel, PhD

As President of Leader's Insight, an Executive Coaching and Leadership Effectiveness consultancy, Dr. Steinwedel provides thought leadership as a consultant and executive coach. She assists leaders in clarifying their goals and objectives and becoming more aware of themselves and their behaviors in service to their aspirations and business results.

With more than 25 years of experience working in such industries as pharmaceuticals, health care, financial services, insurance, engineering, communications, retail, and hospitality, Janet works effectively with a broad range of leaders. She uses an analytical framework which provides a foundational understanding of personality and human behavior—conscious and unconscious processes. In addition to her own work with corporate executives, Janet devotes time to a "coaching for coaches" process in which she helps other executive coaches with their personal and professional development.

Janet is an adjunct professor and speaker, and enjoys travel, playing golf, and spending time with her nieces, nephews, and step-grandchildren.

www.LeadersInsight.com
Twitter: SteinwedelJanet
Facebook: The Golden Key to Executive Coaching

CPSIA information can be obtained
at www.ICGtesting.com
Printed in the USA
BVHW03s0149110818
524077BV00001B/25/P